I DISCOVER
THE ORIENT

I DISCOVER
THE ORIENT

BY
FLETCHER S. BROCKMAN

HARPER & BROTHERS PUBLISHERS
NEW YORK   LONDON

Contents

Acknowledgments

Acknowledgment is hereby made to the following authors and publishers for permission to quote somewhat extensively from their works:

Student Volunteer Movement: *Report of the First International Convention of the Student Volunteer Movement for Foreign Missions*, 1891; *The Student Missionary Enterprise, Addresses and Discussions of the Second International Convention of the Student Volunteer Movement for Foreign Missions*, 1894; and *The Student Missionary Appeal, Addresses of the Third International Convention of the Student Volunteer Movement for Foreign Missions*, 1898;

Fleming H. Revell Company: *Report of the Centenary Congress of Protestant Missions of the World*, held in London, 1888;

Student Volunteer Movement: *The Evangelization of the World in This Generation*, by John R. Mott;

The Baker & Taylor Company: *Expansion under New World Conditions*, by Josiah Strong;

The Board of Foreign Missions of the Presbyterian Church in the U. S. A.: *The Sacred Edict*, F. W. Baller, translator;

Dodd, Mead & Company: *Indiscreet Letters from Peking*, B. L. Putnam Weale, editor;

Fleming H. Revell Company: *China in Convulsion*, by Arthur H. Smith;

Edgar Snow and *New York Herald Tribune*, "Awakening the Masses in China";

Harper & Brothers: *A New Translation of the Bible*, by James Moffatt;

Kegan Paul, Trench, Trubner & Company: *The Development of the Logical Method in Ancient China*, by Hu Shih.

Preface

DURING the past five years the relation of Christianity to other religions has assumed a new and almost passionate interest. Are the non-Christian religions friends or enemies? Do they have values which should be conserved? If so, to what extent may Christianity supplement them, or may they supplement Christianity? Does one find in them elements of truth which are lacking in Christianity? Will the ultimate religion of the world be Christian, or a synthesis of several religions?

We are in no danger of over-estimating the significance of these inquiries. Our appraisal of other faiths means perforce a fresh appraisal of Christianity and raises questions as to the validity of its claim to a world-wide mission. To be conclusive, answers to these questions require an approach from different points of view, and testimony from men of widely varying experience.

It is my purpose in these pages to give my answers to the questions in the light of twenty-five years of missionary effort in the Far East. They are the answers of a practical worker rather than a scholar, given from the standpoint of experience rather than that of philosophy or theology. In order to furnish dependable data for the inquiry, I have tried to make this account of my experience comprehensive, accurate, and objective.

As a check on the conception I held of the Oriental religions and peoples before I sailed for China, I have not only gone carefully through my own private papers, but have reviewed the books which most influenced my thinking and restudied the reports of the conferences and conventions which I attended before I sailed for the Orient.

In describing my early conception of my task and of the culture of the Orient I have not knowingly suppressed any of the evidence. If I seem to be without a sense of shame as I confess my pride of creed, country, and race, my ignorance, insularity, and blindness, this is due to my determination to be honest with the reader.

Any attempt to give an appraisal of the present-day moral and religious values in Confucianist, Buddhist, and Taoist literature lies beyond the scope of this review of my own experience. I have included in an appendix a list of books, kindly prepared by my friend Dr. Arthur W. Hummel, Chief of the Division of Orientalia of the Library of Congress, which will help the reader in making such an appraisal.

In describing my relations with non-Christians I have referred almost exclusively to Confucianists. The explanation of this lies in the fact that the educated classes are overwhelmingly Confucian, and it was with them that I was chiefly associated.

During my first years in China my ideas concerning the relation between Christianity and the non-Christian religions were developed chiefly through my own contacts with the Confucian leaders themselves. As my work became increasingly administrative and consultative, my education progressed largely through my observation and appraisal of enterprises carried forward by my colleagues, and for which I was in some measure responsible.

My experience was wrought out with no little agony of spirit. More than once I was on the verge of abandoning my career. My service covered a period of cataclysmic changes in the Far East. If I were capable of utilizing the dramatic possibilities in the various crises, personal and national, through which I passed, the reader might be held by the same tenseness which gripped me. I have made no attempt to dramatize, but have centered the reader's attention upon the processes which molded my changing conception of the relation between Christianity and the religious heritage of the East.

The circumstances under which the manuscript has been prepared have forced me to make unusual demands upon my friends for assistance. The following have read the manuscript and offered invaluable advice: Mr. Charles H. Fahs, Dr. D. Willard Lyon, Dr. and Mrs. Henry B. Sharman, Dr. Samuel McCrea Cavert, Mrs. Charles F. MacLean, Professor T. M. Campbell, and Mr. Fred I. Eldridge. I have profited greatly by the help of Mr. Henry E.

Wilson in his review of the first eight chapters. From the beginning Mr. E. R. Leibert has acted as a close adviser and has placed at my disposal his intimate knowledge of the Far East and of the work which I have described. I am quite at a loss to enumerate the many kinds of help which I have received from Mrs. Brockman, Miss Edith E. Pelton, and Mr. Milton S. Mulloy. Particularly do I owe them a debt for their untiring zeal and efficiency in research into my correspondence and papers, in preparation and correction of the manuscript, and in reading of the proof.   F. S. B.

New York City,
28th June, 1935.

Chapter I: My Novitiate

In MY infancy my father and mother moved from Virginia to Georgia and settled at Glenwood, a cotton plantation which had belonged to my grandfather, on the Chattahooche River some twenty-five miles from Atlanta. The disintegration of the rural life of the South, caused by the Civil War, was already well advanced and our community afforded almost no educational facilities. Until I was twelve there was no opportunity to go to school except for two or three short sessions taught by my sister, who had returned from college in Virginia. Before that we had studied at home under my mother, who, in spite of frail health, carried the heavy responsibilities imposed by her position as wife of the owner of a large plantation.

One of the earliest recollections of my childhood is the serious concern of my parents over this lack of school facilities for my three brothers and myself. But as I think over what that life on the farm meant to me, I am not certain that any other educational opportunity would have exceeded it in value. While I have felt the lack of early schooling, the experiences on our Georgia plantation were a powerful formative influence in my life and it would not be easy to compensate for their loss. My father and mother had each enjoyed the privilege of a college education, both were earnest Christians, and they made the plantation life itself an education to us.

We were early taught a sense of responsibility. By the time we were eight or nine, each of us had been given a "cotton patch," its size adjusted to our ability to look after it. The heavy work was done by the regular farm laborers, but the planting, hoeing, and picking devolved upon us. The money from the sale of the cotton was ours, and we were encouraged to place it in the bank. We were given dogs, cats, goats, and ponies for our enjoyment and as a means of training us in looking after them. We were taught that it was an honor to gain the affection and confidence of an animal.

Daily prayers morning and evening were a part of the regular routine of our life. When my brothers and I were able to read we took our verses in turn. My father did not easily take part in public religious exercises and was inclined to be reticent even in family prayers. But I have never known a greater master in the art of living.

He made a companion of me while I was still a child. On his long drives to Atlanta or other markets he would take me with him in the buggy, and the conversations on these trips have been among the lasting influences in my life. When the humblest laborer, black or white, greeted him with lifted hat, he always returned the courtesy. "Some people think they are too good to lift their hats to laborers," he would remark to me as we drove on, "but I think I should let no man excel me in courtesy."

"Notice that house," he said once as we were passing what had been an attractive home. "It needs paint; the gate is off the hinges; the fence is out of repair; the lawn is not mowed; everything is ramshackle. The owner drinks whisky." I never needed another temperance lecture.

He could live his Christianity more easily than he could explain it. One of the few times I remember his speaking to me about my own religious experience occurred toward the end of such a buggy trip from Atlanta. He said: "You are very young now and you have had to depend on your mother and me to tell you what is right and wrong. But before long, when you are twelve or so perhaps, you will hear God speak to you and you will realize that you are responsible to him rather than to us. I do not need to tell you how you will know when that hour comes or where the voice comes from. You can't mistake it."

It did not seem strange to me that I had to wait for God to speak to me. This was quite in line with my parents' method of training, which was that of keeping a worthwhile and much-desired goal just ahead. For example, almost from the time I could stand alone I was allowed to ride Kit, the gentle old brood mare imported from Virginia, but I understood that I must wait until I was older before I could ride her spirited son, Bragg (named for

General Braxton Bragg). My father gave me a "claim" on Bragg, with the understanding that when I grew old enough to handle him and take proper care of him, he was to be my very own.

My father had talked with me so naturally and easily that he did not create an expectation of something miraculous or startling in this recognition of God's voice. But I was on the lookout for a new and marked experience. None came. I never experienced conversion as a definite and radical change. The atmosphere of our home was so Christian that I grew up naturally into a Christian life.

When I was about nine years of age a series of meetings was held in the Methodist church in the village near our home. At the close an invitation was extended to those who wished to join. I then recalled my father's words about knowing when God should speak to me. I felt impelled to respond to the invitation, but before giving any expression to the desire I consulted my parents. I was quite young to join even the Methodist Church, and three years younger than the Baptist Church would accept one for membership. But after talking with me both my father and mother approved of my joining. As I have thought about it since I have understood something of why my father's clear conviction that the human spirit could recognize the divine had created in him such a wide tolerance. He believed that God would speak and the hearer would understand God's voice. This to my father's mind gave him no right to judge what God would say to any other person, even to a young and ignorant child. He had assured me that God would speak to me. He did not call in question my experience when it had come much earlier than he had predicted, nor did he doubt that God had spoken because I wished to join the Methodist Church of my mother rather than his own Baptist Church. It would have added much to the fruitfulness of my life had I learned from my father at that time this lesson of reverence for the other man's ability to hear God's voice.

The fact that my father and mother belonged to different denominations did not prevent a deep spiritual fellowship between them nor interfere with a unified religious program for the family. During those days of depression each village church had service only twice during the month, so arranged that there was service in either the Baptist or Methodist church every Sunday. The family worshiped one week in the Baptist church and the next in the Methodist. The Baptist and Methodist ministers alike were frequent guests in our home. The memory of this ideal interdenominational relationship often came to me in later years and was a valuable asset. My own home afforded the proof to me that a profound unity underlay our denominational differences.

My father's humility, simplicity, lack of self-seeking, his concern for the poor and his unselfish living for other people, have been an inspiration to me all of these years. As a highly skilled planter, he continued the tradition of a number of generations of his Virginia ancestors. He taught me that no gentleman would be satisfied merely to keep within the law. "There is a law above the law," he said. I was often reminded of this code of the Southern gentleman when I came to learn, years later, something of the code of the Confucian gentleman. I never knew my father to break that higher law.

The tenants and employees of the farm made a very considerable community, and from my father and mother I learned something of what ought to be the relation between employer and employee. We were one great family. If there was a drought or a freshet and a tenant made less on his land than he had expected, my father took the initiative in equitably adjusting the rent. If there came sickness or other hardship into any family, my parents shared the responsibility with them. Although my father was responsible for the financial outcome, the enterprise of the plantation was in reality mutual.

I learned on the farm to appreciate the negro race. Before my younger brother grew to be a companion, my closest friend was a little negro boy. I never realized that he was black, and I white, until one of the white laborers on the farm laughed at our intimacy. In later years, as I lived in other lands and had to adjust myself to other civilizations, I realized more and more the value of those early relationships in which I learned to know a race different from my own.

The controlling motive of my father and mother in all family plans was the education of their children. When I was twelve they left the farm, at what they knew to be great cost to the family fortune, and moved to Palmetto, Georgia, where elementary schools were available. Later they moved to Atlanta, where we children could attend high school.

Soon after we reached Atlanta Miss Laura Haygood, principal of the girls' high school, interested my mother in a Sunday school located in one of the most neglected portions of the city. She also offered me a class of young boys in the school. I saw a great deal of Miss Haygood during the next eighteen months through our association in the Sunday school and our efforts to help the wretched community in which it was located. Toward the end of this time I learned that she was favorably considering a call to go to China as a missionary. I, a youth of fifteen, boldly and confidently went to her home to persuade her against accepting it. She listened to my argument considerately, and then quietly explained her reasons for going to China. No missionary work had been attempted for higher-class women. There was almost no provision for their education, and custom demanded their living secluded within the inner courts of their homes. The modernization of China, which was bound soon to take place, would find these women unprepared for the new day. She wanted to found a school for high-class girls and to train leaders for the womanhood of the future. I did not succeed in my purpose. Instead, when I left the interview I had a new and startling conception of China as a field of opportunity.

My mother was the daughter of a Methodist preacher. She had but one ambition for her four sons, namely that they should become Christian workers. Her dream came true; of the three who grew to manhood all went as missionaries, one to Korea and two of us to China.

So far as I can recall, my decision to go as a missionary to China was made upon this basis: I have decided to enter the Christian ministry. I should go where the need is greatest. In China there are four hundred million people, most of whom have never heard of Christ even now, two thousand years after his birth. China is open to missionaries. How can I, as a Christian, say I really believe in Christ if I continue to keep the "good news" of him from one-third of the human race?

This decision was made before I entered college. At that time I had never heard of the Student Volunteer Movement. So far as I can recall, I had never seen a missionary nor read a book on missions. The few missionary sermons which I had heard preached before the annual church collection for foreign missionary work, without exception had made a distinctly unfavorable impression upon me.

After finishing my course at the high school I spent two years in teaching before entering Vanderbilt University as a freshman in 1887. Vanderbilt opened a new world to me, for I was thrown at once into intimate association with a group of men on the faculty remarkable in scholarship, religious zeal, enthusiasm for teaching, and charm of personality.

During my college days there were only three Oriental students at Vanderbilt. One of these, Yun Tchi Ho, the son of an exiled Korean nobleman, became a very intimate friend. We lived in the same dormitory and were classmates. He was one of the most popular men in the university, and a noted orator.

Charlie Soong, a Chinese who had been graduated the year before I entered college, was mentioned often on the campus by both students and members of the faculty. He was so much of a tradition that he seemed like an old friend when I met him later in Shanghai.

I entered college just after the birth of the Student Volunteer Movement, and during my student days John Mott, Robert Wilder, and Robert Speer, the outstanding leaders of the movement, visited Vanderbilt. I soon identified myself with it and with them, and during my junior and senior years visited all of the colleges of Tennessee to press upon students a consideration of the needs of non-Christian lands.

Apart from these visitors to Vanderbilt, I recall

but one missionary address which I heard while
there. It was given by Dr. Young J. Allen, editor of
the *International Review of the Times*, president of
the Anglo-Chinese College in Shanghai, and the most
famous missionary of the Southern Methodist
Church. His boyhood home and mine were close together in Georgia. I was, of course, eager to hear
him and know him. His address at Vanderbilt was
masterly, unlike any missionary address I had ever
heard. He spoke on his work for the intelligentsia
of China, and the opportunity for the missionary
to change the currents of thought. He had an ex-
alted opinion of the Chinese people. It was ten years
after I reached China before I was able to measure
the full significance of his address.

Seven years intervened between my graduation in
1891 and my sailing for the field. This whole period
was spent as a national secretary of the Student
Young Men's Christian Association, assigned primarily to work in the colleges and universities of the
Southern States. While in this capacity I was required to give my attention to all aspects of the religious life of the colleges, I gave special attention to
the promotion of interest in foreign missions. And
I made an earnest effort to learn everything I could
about the mission fields. I kept in close touch with
the Student Volunteer Movement and was present
at two of the three conventions held before 1899.
I attended all of the conventions of the Inter-semi-

nary Missionary Alliance, and usually three student conferences each year, held at Northfield, Massachusetts, Lake Geneva, Wisconsin, and Knoxville, Tennessee. I read the current missionary literature, including books and magazines, and came to know missionaries from all of the great mission fields.

My years of preparation were in the geographical and statistical era of the missionary enterprise. The missionary speaker was always equipped with a large map of the world on which the Christian countries were marked in white and the heathen in black. This map was hung behind the speaker, who was able with a long pointer to carry his audience from nation to nation and drive home the overwhelming size of the task which lay before the Christian Church.

"They [the heathen] include 850,000,000," said the secretary of one of the missionary boards in his address before the first International Convention of the Student Volunteer Movement. "They include the greater part of the population of Asia . . . Africa, considerable portions of the population of America and the islands of the sea. . . . As the eye passes from continent to continent, from nation to nation, and from people to people and we recall they are heathen, 200,000,000; these are heathen, 250,000,000; these are heathen, 350,000,000; . . . more than half of the population of the globe are in midnight gloom. . . .

"They know not the God we worship . . . having no hope and without God in the world. They are there today; they are in China today, they are in Japan today by the million and the hundred million without a ray of the light that shines on us. . . . Life has for them no future that can inspire desire. Life has for them no aim that can lift up. Heaven they know not."[1]

At the next convention of the Student Volunteer Movement, in 1894, I was greatly impressed by an address from which I select a few sentences:

"Why should I go to China? . . . One reason is because a million a month in that great land are dying without God. Can you picture what it is to die without God? Can you imagine it? . . .

"Another reason, because 300,000,000 in China are living without God. O brothers and sisters, can you picture what it is to live without God? Have you ever thought of it, to have no hope for the future and none for the present, to have no refuge in our sorrows and cares, to have no heart of love to turn to in bereavement and loss, to have no stronger arm than our own to lean upon, to have no light at all upon the great beyond?"[2]

Of course, such descriptions were not the result of careful investigation of religious conditions. In fact,

[1] *Report of the First International Convention of the Student Volunteer Movement for Foreign Missions*, 1891, pp. 134-136. Student Volunteer Movement, New York City.

[2] Max Wood Moorhead, ed., *The Student Missionary Enterprise, Addresses and Discussions of the Second International Convention of the Student Volunteer Movement for Foreign Missions*, 1894, pp. 239-240. Student Volunteer Movement, New York City.

there was a distinct prejudice against a study of the non-Christian religions.

"Now I know that I may arouse a little prejudice," said a board secretary of one of the larger missionary societies in his address before an international convention of the Student Volunteer Movement, "when I say we must study the heathen systems which we are to encounter. . . . I would not advise missionaries to give much time to the study of these systems, but I wish there might be put into the hands of every missionary a well-prepared little tract with just the concrete pith of the argument against all these lines of attack, against all these allegations of Buddhism and Atheism and Hinduism. We must have some idea of these things; we must know where the main points are; we cannot go out as ignoramuses. Do not learn the heathen systems for your own sake, but find out their inconsistencies and enormities and absurdities, that you place instead of these the true word as it is in Jesus Christ."[1]

Thus, as my preparation for missionary service progressed, I was put on my guard against "a tendency to idealize the condition of the heathen and the heathen world"[2] and against the seductive influence of the non-Christian faiths, especially Confucianism, which emphasized the importance of morality.

[1] *Report of the First International Convention of the Student Volunteer Movement for Foreign Missions,* 1891, pp. 119-120. Student Volunteer Movement, New York City.

[2] *Ibid.,* p. 136.

One of the speakers in the second Cleveland Convention of the Student Volunteer Movement, in discussing a most serious problem confronting the missionary dealing with Confucianists, said: "I refer to the magnificent ideas concerning ethics which obtain among the adherents of Confucius . . . we are to remember that just in proportion as a system approaches truth, that system becomes a dangerous counterfeit. You are therefore to be pitted against a very close semblance of truth, and must deal with excellences which are to be acknowledged. The Confucianist, blind to spiritual truths, will not much desire a Christianity which, according to his conception, is so little superior to his own system."[1]

As most of those who spoke or wrote about missionary work were more familiar with the Bible than with the conditions in foreign countries they used the Old and New Testaments, especially the Old, as their source books on religious life in heathen lands. The passage most frequently used to describe the people in non-Christian lands was from Paul's letter to the Romans: "And even as they did not like to retain God in their knowledge, God gave them over to a reprobate mind, to do those things which are not convenient; being filled with all unrighteousness, fornication, wickedness, covetousness, maliciousness; full of envy, murder, debate, deceit, malignity;

[1] *The Student Missionary Appeal, Addresses at the Third International Convention of the Student Volunteer Movement for Foreign Missions,* 1898, p. 96. Student Volunteer Movement, New York City.

whisperers; backbiters, haters of God, despiteful, proud, boasters, inventors of evil things, disobedient to parents, without understanding, covenant-breakers, without natural affection, implacable, unmerciful."[1]

I, too, turned often to my heroes among the Old Testament prophets, Elijah, Amos, Isaiah, and Ezra, and studied their courageous and uncompromising conflict with heathenism. And I made them my models for my future work in the Orient.

[1] Romans 1:28-32 (Authorized Version).

Chapter II: Daylight Opens the City Gate

As a result of my rather long novitiate, what was my conception of the foreign missionary's task and what progress had I made in a knowledge of the Chinese whom I expected to serve? As I look back on it now, after nearly forty years, the conception of my missionary task at that time was a tangle of many strands, all of which I considered of equal value. The next ten years were largely taken up with discovering and untangling the true from the false without destroying my sense of mission. I was ignorant of the history, religion, philosophy, and customs of the Chinese. I had formed the habit of looking for the bad in China; this included all that was bad in social, political, and industrial conditions, as well as in individuals. Perhaps it would have been almost as tragic to be on the lookout only for the good. But appreciation—an open door to the good—is essential to an understanding of any people, including our own. In this I was almost totally lacking.

From the standpoint of the religious need of the mission field, I looked upon all of the non-Christian countries as presenting the same problem. They were composed of heathen, and at the distance from which

I viewed them all heathen were alike. I believed sincerely that all the non-Christian religions should be destroyed root, stock, and branch. As I anticipated my work in China I remembered my father's remark when he was clearing two swamps on the plantation in Georgia in my boyhood. He said to me: "You can tell a good planter from a poor one by the thoroughness with which he clears a swamp." His method of clearing required much extra expense and time; all stumps were dug up; the uttermost roots of the bramble briers were searched out and destroyed; the brush was burned; and the land was allowed to mellow before the corn was planted. I determined to keep my father's example in mind in dealing with heathen customs and religions. The religious leaders of China were hostile to Christianity, I thought, and I must meet them with the same spirit. It was to be a fight to the finish between light and darkness.

The attitude of conflict so prevalent in the foreign missionary enterprise at that time usually clothed itself in military rather than agricultural terminology. These are typical quotations:

"Christians must go to the front. How is it a captain leads his company into the battle?"[1]

"Why should we expend our resources for missions? . . . It is a fight for life. We have got to conquer them, or they will conquer us."[2]

[1] *Report of the Centenary Congress of Protestant Missions of the World,* held in London, 1888, vol. ii, p. 510. Fleming H. Revell, New York.

[2] *Ibid.,* vol. i, p. 323.

"Although breaches are being made in the walls of the non-Christian religions, they still manifest great powers of resistance. The increasing success of Christianity in all parts of the world has seemed to arouse them to renewed activity and vigor. This intensifies the conflict involved in the evangelization of the world in this generation."[1]

It was but one step from thinking of missionary work as a war against heathenism to interpreting the victories of Christian nations against non-Christian nations as victories of God against his enemies. Now it is difficult for us to realize to what an extent this ideology prevailed before 1914. It comes down to us from the long past. Western Christianity inherits it not only through its pagan and barbaric ancestry, but through the Jews, the Greeks, and the Romans who are its cultural forbears.

In order to remind the reader of the interpretation given by Christians of my generation to the expansion of Europe and America into the Near East, the Far East, and Africa, I am giving at some length quotations from missionary leaders. These pronouncements were made by great leaders in delegated bodies and were received without protest. They represented the opinions of many, if not most, Christians. To informed leaders of the Orient these statements were clear evidence of the close relation-

[1] *The Evangelization of the World in This Generation,* John R. Mott, p. 36, Student Volunteer Movement, New York. 1904.

ship between missionary work and the imperialism of the so-called Christian countries.

At the World Congress of Missions referred to above, President Post of the Syrian Protestant College in an address on Syria in its relations to Central Asia and Central Africa, said:

"At the head of the Christian religion, in its pure and reformed shape, is our own Anglo-Saxon race. . . . At the head of the Mohammedan religion is the Arabic race. . . .

"Now it is very remarkable that these two races have certain common characteristics. In the first place, they are great colonizing races; in the second place, they are migratory. *They are not content with colonizing on their mere borders, but they spread all over the world; and they are great conquering races —military races—inclined to conquest. Wherever they put their feet they stay; and wherever they stay they hold the country with a grasp of iron.*[1] It is very remarkable, also, that they share the empire of the world in a very peculiar manner. . . .

"And now mark the providence of God. God has brought the Arabic and the Anglo-Saxon races side by side in the very center of their joint possessions on the coast of Syria, and at the lower portion of the valley of the Nile. Is it fortuitous that in these days of the revival of missionary activity God should have brought the English branch of the Anglo-Saxon race

[1] The italics used in quotations are the author's.

and given it a hold of the two wrists of the Arabic power? You [the English] have planted your standard in the island of Cyprus, you have planted it in Alexandria and along the valley of the Nile, and you hold the Arabic race in the very center, the very keystone of its power and influence, and you control its forces. That alone would be remarkable; but without any such plan as this, and feeling the leadings of the providence of God, the Americans have been led to plant mission stations along that Syrian coast, from Mersin down to the borders of Palestine, and originally, also, throughout Palestine—for the first missions to Jerusalem were by Americans—and also in the valley of the Nile. The English hold the hands— the physical forces; and God has given to the other branch of the Anglo-Saxon race, untrammeled by your political complications, a control of the brain and of the heart. We have been made the educators and the evangelizers of that people. It happens that your peculiar position, your peculiar political complications, might make it difficult for you to fulfill that mission. God knew that before we knew it, and He put us there into the evangelistic and educational work because we could do it. And then in the fullness of time, and when His purposes were ripe, *He brought you with your fleets, and with your cannon, and with your physical forces to hold these people until they could be educated and evangelized.* Do I read aright the purposes of God's providence in reference, then, to Syria and to Egypt in their relation to the great Arabian race in Asia and in Africa?"[1]

Before the same conference another American speaker said:

"We are observing the Centenary of Modern Missions. But the most amazing results of this century have been wrought during its last third, or the lifetime of the generation now living. This World's Conference is simply the Church coming together at the Antioch of the Occident, to hear those whom the Holy Ghost has chosen and the Church has separated unto this work, rehearse all that God has done with them, and how He has opened the door of faith unto the Gentiles. Who dares to say, in the light of Modern Missions, that the days of supernatural working are passed? So far as in primitive days the disciples have gone forth and preached everywhere, it has still been true that the Lord has wrought with and confirmed the Word with signs following—signs unmistakable and unmistakably supernatural. Doors have been opened within fifty years that no human power could have unbarred. *The mighty moving of God can be traced back through the centuries, long since giving Protestant England a foothold in the very critical center, the pivotal center of Oriental empires and religions. The necessity of protecting her Indian possessions, of keeping open the line of communication between London and Calcutta, determined the atti-*

[1] *Report of the Centenary Congress of Protestant Missions of the World,* held in London, 1888, vol. i, pp. 320-323.

tude of every nation along the water highway. Then from beyond the Pacific another mighty, puissant people, the offspring of Protestant Britain, moved forward thirty years ago to turn the extreme eastern wing of the enemy, while Britain was piercing and holding the center. Commodore Perry knocked at the sea gates of Japan, and in the name of a Christian republic demanded entrance. Rusty bolts that had not been drawn for more than two centuries were flung back, and the two-leaved doors of brass were opened to the commerce of the world. Rapid has been the progress of the march of God. Japan unsealed her gates in 1854. From that time not a year has passed without some mighty onward movement or stupendous development. The year 1856 saw signed and sealed the Hatti Sherif in Turkey, by which the Sultan, at least in form, announced the era of toleration. The next year the mutiny in India changed the whole attitude of the East India Company toward missions, and prepared the way for the surrender of its charter to the Crown of England. *In 1858 the great breach was made in the Chinese wall, and by the treaty of Tientsin one-third of the human race were made accessible to Christian nations; and, as Dr. Gracey says, that wide door was opened, not by the vermilion pencil of the Emperor, but by the decree of the Eternal.*

"Let us leap the chasm of twenty years, and note the progress of events on the Dark Continent. In

1871 Stanley pierced the jungles to find the heroic Livingstone, who in 1873 died near Lake Bangweolo; in 1874 Stanley undertook to explore Equatorial Africa; in 1877, after a thousand days, he emerged at the mouth of the Congo. At once England took up the work of following the steps of the explorer with the march of the missionary, and now, ten years later, the missions of the great lakes in the east, and those of the Congo Basin at the west, are stretching hands to link east and west together; give us ten years more and Krapf's prophecy will be fulfilled—a chain of missions will cross the continent. In 1884 fifteen nations, called together by King Leopold and presided over by Bismarck, met in Berlin to lay the basis of the Congo Free State; and in that council, not only Protestant, but Greek, Papal, and Moslem powers joined!

"Such are some of the great providential signs of a supernatural Presence and Power."[1]

Dr. Josiah Strong put even more accurately our American feeling as it developed after the War with Spain:

"The stupendous struggle of the future will be not simply between two Titanic races, but between Eastern and Western civilization. . . . For the Russian is an Asiatic who has absorbed Western learning, has mastered Western military science, and who now,

---

[1] *Report of the Centenary Congress of Protestant Missions of the World,* held in London, 1888, vol. ii, pp. 490-492.

without loosening his hold in Europe, is returning to Asia, there to work out his destiny . . . and the genius of the race and its geographical position unite to stimulate its purpose of eastward and southward expansion. Russia can wait, but never vacillates in her supreme purpose. . . . The United States and Russia . . . these two colossal powers will face each other across the arena of the Pacific. Which of the two will command the sea? . . . Is the Anglo-Saxon or the Slav to command the Pacific and therefore the world's future? Consider Hawaii . . . Captain Mahan, the recognized authority of the world on naval warfare and strategy . . . wrote: 'It is rarely that so important a factor in the attack or defense of a coast line is concentrated in a single position.' . . . And as if to leave nothing to be desired, nature provided Hawaii with Pearl Harbor, to which Admiral Walker says: 'It should not be forgotten that Pearl Harbor offers, strategically and otherwise, the finest site for a naval and coaling station to be found in the whole Pacific.' Turn now to the Philippines. They lie at the gateway of China and in the pathway of Oriental commerce.

"Unless prevented by Russia, England and America will give to China the blessings of European civilization, the triumph of which represents the liberation of the individual, not only politically, but religiously and intellectually. Bring the East thoroughly under the influence of the West, and it would be impregnated with a new life. Asia would gain political and religious regeneration; while the world would gain a new literature, a new art, and a new member of the sisterhood of nations.

"If Russia gains control, Asia will remain Asiatic for centuries to come, China's vast resources will become the resources of the Slav, her millions his millions, with their power multiplied many fold by his military skill and his genius for organization. . . .

"Does it seem to any that the lands surrounding this vast ocean [the Pacific] are so far distant from each other as to make the possibility either of conflict or coöperation too remote for serious consideration? Then remember that ever since time became the measure of distance, the Pacific has gradually shrunk until now it is only one-half as large as the Mediterranean was in the days of Classic Greece. . . .

"Turn again to the map. There are six Anglo-Saxon families, all of which are to be numerous and strong—Great Britain, South Africa, the United States, Canada, Australia, and New Zealand. Four of the six are ranged around the Pacific. . . . Surely this New Mediterranean, which in the twentieth century is to be the center of the world's population and the seat of its power, is to be an Anglo-Saxon sea, provided only we place on it an adequate navy. . . . It follows, therefore, that a navy strong enough to cope with the navies of the world would protect Anglo-Saxondom from all the armies of the world.

. . . The Anglo-Saxon families are so placed in the
world that they can defend themselves, command the
Pacific, and accomplish their mission in behalf of
civilization by means of sea power, which may be increased to any required degree of strength in perfect
harmony with their free institutions.

"And has all this no providential meaning? If God
has any interest in human affairs, is it not in progress
and in civil and religious liberty? When we consider
the part which the Pacific is to play in the world's
future, how shall we account for the wholly exceptional relations which the Anglo-Saxons sustain to
it? . . .

"As there are forces at work in human affairs which
are mightier than human power, so there is an intelligence higher than human knowledge, which is
guiding human destinies. The fact that Anglo-Saxons
laid hold of what proved to be the best portions of
the earth—lands which command the commerce, the
population, and the power of the world's future, and
lands which are defended from invasion by nature—
was not due to the foresight of any man or of any
number of men. . . .

"But somehow, notwithstanding the lack of human foresight, notwithstanding human blindness and
opposition, these many different lands, belonging to
many different nations, are found, in a great world
crisis, in the hands of one great race, upon which
they confer decisive power.

"If there is no God in such history, there is no God anywhere. . . ."[1]

If I have nauseated the reader with these lengthy quotations, I have done so intentionally: without such evidence one would find it hard to believe today that at the turn of the century Nationalism screamed, blatant and unashamed, from pulpit and press; that imperialism and self-righteousness marched so openly under Christian banners. Certain it is that doctrine of the sort quoted above could scarcely be received with glad acceptance by its victims.

In my preparation for my missionary career there would seem to have been very few elements omitted which would unfit me for the task. I wish to make clear, however, that there were other elements in my preparation for which I am thankful. I owe a great debt to the Student Volunteer Movement. From the beginning it commanded the services of a wise and brilliant coterie of university students whose future careers have borne out the promises of those days. Although a movement of students, it worked out its program from the beginning in close coöperation with the officers of the missionary societies. The Movement was a reaction against the sense of lethargy into which the Church had fallen as a result of Amer-

[1] Josiah Strong, *Expansion Under New World Conditions,* pp. 191-213. The Baker & Taylor Co., New York, 1900.

ica's period of isolation and consequent ignorance of the rest of the world.

That the Student Volunteer Movement should have become, in a measure, the victim of the very conditions which it was striving to correct, was inevitable. Its leaders saw clearly its duty, realized the size and urgency of its task and the consequent demand for divine assistance, but they were so absorbed in the *ought* that they gave scant attention to the *how*.

Although family responsibilities delayed my going to the field seven years after the completion of my university course, my fellowship with kindred spirits, the conventions and conferences at which the missionary obligation was emphasized, and my own efforts under the Student Volunteer Movement to promote missionary interest among students, were invaluable factors in reinforcing my original sense of mission. Through these influences this sense of mission grew to an overwhelming compulsion.

The Movement rendered me a great service also in the note of urgency which it continuously sounded during the first decade of its existence. It is true that the motto, "The Evangelization of the World in This Generation," was misinterpreted by some shallow and over-enthusiastic persons, but what it did for me was to drive home two thoughts: first, you are responsible to your generation; and second, what you are to do for your generation must be done now.

Again, I am thankful for the emphasis which was

placed upon the supernatural aspect of the missionary task. It is not good form to use such language now—I am aware of that. But I am writing in the light of many years of experience, and I regard as an indispensable factor in my preparation the realization that the work was beyond human power to accomplish. The task looked big and difficult to me before I sailed for China. The geographical and statistical form in which it had been described to me made it formidable enough. But, by contrast, the reality of its infinite complexity and difficulty made my original conceptions childishly simple and easy.

Mrs. Brockman and I, with our two-year-old son, sailed for China on the *Empress of India* early in October, 1898. In those days China was remote, and even important news traveled slowly. In August, two months before our departure, the Emperor had been dethroned and made a prisoner by the Empress Dowager, jealous of his growing power among the people. It now seems incredible that an occurrence of such significance to the world should not have appeared in great headlines in all the leading newspapers of Europe and America, but no word of this momentous event reached us until we arrived in Japan. It was an event of first importance in the history of China—the elimination of the only element which could have enabled China to make an orderly adjustment from an ancient to a modern state.

Within a period of three months before his dethronement the Emperor had issued a series of reform edicts which for thoroughness, brilliance, and
comprehensiveness startled all students of Chinese
affairs. They recommended an immediate modernization of the entire life of the nation. If the program
of the Emperor could have been carried through,
China might have entered the new era, as did Japan,
without injury to the structure of her civilization.
The Empress Dowager, however, represented the reactionary forces of the Manchu régime, and the Emperor's downfall spelled the victory of the reactionaries over the reformers.

Our first sight of Chinese soil awakened in us a
startling realization of the threat which the great
powers of the world gave to China. As we sailed into
Shanghai harbor we saw battleships, cruisers, and
other craft flying the flags of seemingly every large
European nation. The one flag conspicuous for its
absence was that of China. The forest of the masts
of Chinese junks, a Yangtze River steamer and a
swarm of sampans provided the only local atmosphere
to indicate that we were in a Chinese port.

We were welcomed at the jetty by my colleagues,
D. Willard Lyon and Robert E. Lewis, and were
taken to the home of Miss Laura Haygood for our
stay in Shanghai. I early sought out Charlie Soong.
I found him so quiet and unpretentious that I won-
dered at the impression which he had made upon the

students and faculty at Vanderbilt. But as our friendship grew I came to discover in him the qualities
which had so endeared him to friends in America.
We became intimate friends, but it was years later
before I learned that he was then the financial head
of Sun Yat-sen's revolutionary efforts. In this capacity he silently carried a staggering burden for
years. At that time neither he nor I dreamed of the
powerful influence which his family was later to exert
in the political life of China.

I also called upon Dr. Young J. Allen—a most
impressive figure, tall, with white hair and long
white beard. His eyes greeted me with kindly interest,
but bore the mark of the wide sweep of his thought.
Often in the years which were to follow I made pil-
grimages to his study, and came to think of it as a
dynamo from which emanated influences that spread
to all the best minds of China. I never left an interview with him without inspiration and fresh courage.

I had been in Shanghai but a brief time before I
learned that the division of China among the European nations and Japan was taken for granted and
seemed imminent. Almost everyone with whom I
talked considered it an accomplished fact in all but
name. With amazing rapidity Russia was building
the Siberian Railway from Moscow to the Gulf of
Pechili. Talienwan, or Dalny, its eastern terminus,
was to be made the model port of the world. Their
ablest engineers and architects had planned every
detail of its erection, including provisions for parks,

gardens, theaters and bazaars. The Tsar was supplying, without question, the huge funds necessary.

With equal haste and even greater efficiency Germany was proceeding with the development of the strategic center of Tsingtao.

As a foil to Russia and Germany, England had taken the port of Wei-hai-wei, and had increased by two hundred square miles her territory adjacent to Hongkong. Just before we reached Shanghai Lord Beresford of the British Admiralty had arrived there. As head of the British Chambers of Commerce, he was meeting with British merchants in the different cities of China to discuss with them the readjustment of British trade in the light of the threatened division of China among the nations. After his return to England, Lord Beresford's report was published under the significant title, *The Break-up of China*.

France had demanded a port in South China and was reported to have marked for her own the large island of Hainan.

Japan, it was conceded, would be given the Province of Fukien.

Before we reached Shanghai arrangements had been made for me to make a tour of the Christian colleges in Hongkong, Swatow, Amoy, Foochow, Shanghai, and Nanking. This delayed by two months my study of the language; but it was a valuable experience, for it gave me an opportunity to meet at the beginning of my work a considerable number of English-speaking Chinese professors, students, and business men. Their intelligence, alertness, and earnestness made a most favorable impression upon me.

In the first letter which I wrote back to New York I announced my surrender of any sense of Anglo-Saxon superiority over the Chinese. But I was surprised and disappointed at their attitude toward the threatened break-up of their country. When I inquired of certain Chinese whom I had learned to know well enough to ask such a question, they seemed unaware of the significance of what the foreign countries were doing. I could forgive such an attitude in the poor coolie who pulled my jinricksha, but how could intelligent men be so blind or so unfeeling?

I rationalized their attitude in this way: Granted that intellectually the Chinese are not inferior to the Europeans, there must be something lacking in Chinese character or they would resent this rape of their own country. Such indifference must be an inheritance of heathenism.

This judgment was soon to be proven false by the Boxer outbreak, in which even the coolies showed an uninformed but flaming patriotism.

During the first days of January, 1899, Mrs. Brockman and I took a river steamer for Nanking, which had not at that time become an open port. There were no wharves and none but the crudest facilities for the landing of passengers. We arrived one midnight in a cold drizzle at Hsiakwan, a small group of adobe huts outside the North Gate of Nanking. A coolie, bearing a letter from Professor Bowen of the Anglo-Chinese College, boarded the boat. The note explained that the city gates were locked after nine o'clock at night, and that this would necessitate our waiting outside the wall until they were opened again shortly after daybreak.

We were set ashore in deep mud and all our earthly possessions were piled on the bank. We walked to a near-by adobe hut for shelter. In the middle of its dirt floor the coolie placed a charcoal brazier over which Mrs. Brockman and our small son hovered and shivered while we waited for daylight. The city wall rose sixty feet above us in the darkness. It seemed to me that the giant doors of the city gate, locked and barred, were a symbol of the hearts of the people within the walls.

We were at the end of our long journey—the goal of twelve years of waiting, hoping, and striving. Our dreams had come true; we had no doubt of that, even though the reality lacked the glamour of the dreams.

At dawn the gates were opened, and soon we were welcomed into one of the most charming missionary groups I have ever known. The warmth of their greeting, and the depth of their fellowship which the ensuing years revealed, fill me with gratitude even now as I write these lines.

Chapter III: An Emperor Is My Teacher

LANGUAGE study began immediately with Ma *Sien Seng*, a Mohammedan, as my teacher. He was rather slender and of medium height, with an intellectual face. His manner was reserved, but he was kindly and patient with my slowness to learn. I soon came to appreciate him highly.

After some six months of elementary study we began reading together the *Sacred Edict*. It was one of the few books at that time available in the colloquial language and easily understood by the common people. In its original form it consisted of sixteen maxims written in the highest literary style by the Emperor K'ang Hsi in 1670, and later was published in an enlarged form with an exposition in colloquial style. For many years it had been printed by the government in great quantities and distributed free or at a nominal cost. No other document was so widely read or had such an influence upon the common people. In every city and town of the country it was read publicly twice a month. In it a kindly monarch talks in an intimate way with his people on a wide range of subjects. Among other things he discusses farming and mulberry culture, thrift and economy, schools and academies, courtesy, and human relationships.

My first lesson in the *Sacred Edict* was on Family Relationships. I was to read each passage after my teacher and catch as accurately as possible his way of saying it. Then I was to memorize it. Here is part of that first day's reading:

"Duty to parents is a self-evident principle of nature, and the root of virtuous conduct in man.

"You who are children, and do not know how to do your duty by your parents, only think of their passionate affection for you and see whether you ought to be filial or not.

"When you were a babe in arms, were you hungry? You could not feed yourself. Cold? You could not clothe yourself. Your parents looked upon your face, listened to your voice. Did you laugh, they were pleased. Did you cry, they were sad. Did you toddle, step by step they followed you. If you had never so trifling an ailment they were distressed to the last degree and could not take their food.

"They looked forward with great expectation to your coming to manhood. You do not know how much fatigue they endured; how much anxiety they bore to rear you and to instruct you.

"Just think: You were born a little naked being and did not bring a stitch of silk or cotton with you. Up till now you have had food and clothing through your parents' kindness. Can you ever repay them?"[1]

[1] F. W. Baller, trans., *The Sacred Edict,* fourth edition, revised, pp. 2-3. China Inland Mission and Presbyterian Mission Press, Shanghai, 1917.

After this lesson was over and Mr. Ma had gone, I tried to picture the Emperor who was on such intimate and fatherly terms with his people. I could imagine no President whom we had had in America talking like that. And the Chinese home which he described was one that I had supposed inconceivable in a heathen land. I resolved that when I was farther along with the language I would get Mr. Ma to answer some of the questions that the day's lesson had raised.

We next came to the passages on Recompense to Parents:

"Now the performance of duty to parents is no impossibility; it is merely to put their minds at rest and to care for their bodies. How put their minds at rest? At home in the ordinary course of things do good and be good.

"How should you minister to their bodily wants? To the extent of your ability, to the limit of your means, sedulously cherish the aged couple. Rather eat less and use less yourself, that they may have all they want to eat and to use.

"On no account go gambling and drinking. On no account fight with others."[1]

All of this was quite inconsistent with my conception of Chinese life. I turned to the Preface of the edition which I was using, edited for young missionaries by a senior missionary whom I highly honored, and found this warning against thinking too highly of what I would find in the text:

[1] *Ibid.*, pp. 4-5.

"The *Sacred Edict* is useful as giving a comprehensive view of Chinese life and character, and showing the value of mere moral teaching. In every chapter may be seen the importance attached by this people to respect to parents and seniors, and deference to rulers;—principles which probably have done much toward securing that long continuance as a nation, of which China is justly proud: but the only true source of right action, the recognition of man's responsibility to God, is unknown—almost unhinted at."[1]

For a time these words quieted my misgivings.

Within a few days we came to the theme of the Duties of Brothers to One Another:

"Besides your parents there are your brothers. These brothers must not be looked on as separable the one from the other. He and I are one flesh and blood, and are therefore spoken of as 'Hands and Feet.' If you treat your brother badly, you are really slighting your parents.

"All the squabbles that arise among brethren in the present day are on account of property. Some squabble about money, some about land, some about houses, some about food: all sorts of things. But they overlook the fact that monetary affairs are trifling compared with the weighty affections of kith and kin. What if there is a little unfairness in dividing the family estate, the advantage is still in the family.

[1] *Ibid.*, Preface, p. v.

"Think a little—wealth is a flowing commodity; if it goes, there is more to be had."[1]

From the family we turned in several weeks' time to a study of the District Community:

"From time immemorial there have been district communities. Why called communities? Well, for example, the near and distant neighbors in every village and hamlet are the inhabitants of such village or hamlet. Their fields adjoin, their houses touch, they meet as they go in and out, they hear each other's fowls and dogs, they intermarry, they render mutual aid in case of fire, flood, or robbery—which of them do you suppose is not very intimate with his neighbor?

"So then, among the inhabitants of this our hamlet, treat them all kindly, and in all things, important or trivial, be ready to give way. If there be calamity, by all means render assistance; if sickness, by all means call and ask after the patient; if there be litigation, exert yourself to the utmost to bring about a reconciliation, and do not help on the quarrel by talebearing; if there be a robbery or a fire, combine to give assistance: do not take pleasure in calamity.

"Take, for instance, the case of a poor villager. I ought to assist him; in a debt of many years' standing that cannot be repaid, the thing to do is to let him off on generous terms.

"In the case of a simple-minded or easy-going

[1] *Ibid.,* pp. 8, 11, 12, 14.

neighbor, you must treat him fairly with the strictest impartiality.

"As regards the wealthy resident, if at some time or other you have borrowed something of his to help you in an emergency, it is only right and proper to return it promptly at the appointed time.

"In the case of an ill-disposed neighbor, seek to influence him for good. You should give way to him in all things, be very patient with him.

"In conclusion, if anyone has shown a lack of courtesy to you, just excuse him, and not be as undiscerning as he. Or suppose a person, destitute of common sense, treats you rudely or insults you, be content with bringing reason to bear on him and in no wise lay it to heart.

"The ancients rightly said, 'He who can swallow an affront is the true man'; and again, 'If when another hates me I do not hate him, enmity will cease at once.' What if another is quarrelsome? *You* simply concern yourself with keeping the peace—one foolish, the other wise. If he sees you are long-suffering he will come to a better mind.

"Always be ready to pocket an affront, and nobody will say you are simple, but all will love you. Is not this position in which you suffer loss the position in which you really gain advantage? Hence the ancients, in changing their residences, did not seek for good houses, but only for good neighbors.

"If people would regard all connected with the community as making one corporate body, if there were advantages all would enjoy them; if adversities, all share them: this would be true union among the people."[1]

One day some scandal arose in the city concerning the Viceroy's soldiers, and Mr. Ma referred rather contemptuously to soldiers as a class. As courteously as my limited language would permit, I suggested to him that it was unfortunate that China should despise her soldiers.

"This," I continued, "accounts for the fact that she does not get her best men to go into the army. With us in America it is very different. Our greatest men have often been soldiers. Our first President, George Washington, was the head of our army."

"Yes," he replied, "we passed that stage in our civilization a thousand years ago. You honor the man with a short coat and a sword buckled on; we honor the man with a long robe and a pen in his hand."

After he left, I thought over the incident. There was something incongruous in the situation. When Mr. Ma was recommended to me, I had hesitated to employ him, on the ground that he was a Mohammedan. I had thought of him as the representative of a religion that was warlike, and of myself as a representative of the Prince of Peace. But now he, a Mohammedan, was condemning war, while I, a Christian, defended it!

As I studied further I was surprised to find strong

[1] *Ibid.*, pp. 29, 31-37.

denunciation of idolatry. In America I had pictured the fight against the worship of idols as one of my main duties. But I found that China's greatest Emperor had begun this fight more than two hundred years before I reached the country. All through the *Sacred Edict* were passages on this theme bearing the prestige of the mighty ruler's name. The Emperor had tried to be fair to the teachings of the Buddhist and Taoist and to recognize the good done by them, but in the following quotation I found a stronger condemnation of the personnel of the priesthood and their practices than I could ever have hoped to make.

"All this talk about fasts, getting up processions, building temples and making idols, is invented by loafing idle Buddhist and Taoist priests as a plan for swindling you. Yet forsooth you will believe them, and not only go yourself to burn incense and worship at the temple, but let your wives and daughters enter the temples to burn incense; with oiled hair and powdered faces, gaily dressed, to shoulder and elbow, and crowd and jostle with these Taoist and Buddhist priests and riffraff! Where the 'practising goodness' comes in nobody knows, but many disgraceful things are done, provoking to anger and vexation, and causing others to ridicule.

"Now these villainous Buddhist and Taoist priests are a parcel of lazy bones.

"As to Taoists. They drive away spirits and chase away the General, destroy apparitions and expel noxious influences, call to the wind, summon the rain, and worship the Dipper. It is needless to say it is all a pack of lies."[1]

The great Emperor disapproved also of the Roman Catholics who had been working in China since the thirteenth century. He dealt with them briefly in the following statement:

"Neither are the Papists orthodox, who speak of heaven and earth, and the Invisible. It was simply because they understood astronomy and were able to calculate the rules for astronomical tables, that the government made use of them to compile the Calendar. This is by no means to say their sect is good; you must on no account believe them."[2]

This supercilious attitude toward the priests who had given help in astronomy and other branches of science had behind it the story of a dispute between the Pope and K'ang Hsi, the Emperor. The Pope had declared that the rites involved in ancestral worship were idolatrous. K'ang Hsi had maintained they were civil and in no way religious. He deeply resented the fact that a private citizen in a little country of Europe should presume to tell the people of China that their Emperor was wrong in a matter of Chinese interpretation.

The study of the *Sacred Edict* had enlightened me regarding the character of the Chinese, their moral teachings, their human relationships, and their opposition to idolatry. It had raised questions in my mind, but I did not then try to answer them.

[1] *Ibid.,* pp. 79, 83.
[2] *Ibid.,* pp. 84-85.

Chapter IV: The Baptism of Fire

I HAD expected, upon arrival in Nanking, to be absorbed and undisturbed in the one task of language study. But it soon became clear, even to me as a newcomer, that conditions in the country were not normal. One gained the impression of a situation strange and complex with an undertone distinctly ominous. The city was filled with famine refugees who had poured in by the thousands from the northern border of the province. It was the second year of complete crop failure in that region and the refugees had come to Nanking, where an imperial granary was located. They were given a daily "dole" by order of the Viceroy, but they had brought practically nothing with them from their homes and their condition was heartbreaking. They camped outside the city walls, where they had built a town of frail shacks, using for their construction the reeds which grew in abundance in the river marshes.

Each day when the city gates were opened practically the whole population of the refugee camp—men, women, and children, started to move on the six-mile journey to the granary. They were the aged and young, the lame, halt, and blind—in fact, everyone who was able to walk, with some carrying babies in arms or in baskets suspended from both ends of carrying-poles. At certain hours of the day they filled the streets.

Parents offered their children for sale for a few pennies, and more than once Mrs. Brockman and I were urged by a mother to buy her child in order to save its life. We found not infrequently that we had no appetite for dinner when we returned home after a walk through the city. In one afternoon we would see more misery than we had witnessed in all the rest of our lives before coming to China.

Disquieting reports were reaching us almost daily as to conditions within the district from which the refugees had come. The whole region was infested with thieves and robbers. The government was not taking adequate steps either to maintain order or to deal with the economic conditions. At Woyang, a small city in the neighboring province of Anhui, a rebellion had broken out, with the insurgents numbering several thousand. A few weeks later trouble appeared at a point just a little farther north. This was of such a serious nature that the government considered it wise to order troops from Tientsin to quell the insurrection, even though it would take them a month to reach the center of disturbance.

As the spring of 1899 approached, the center of the uprisings shifted north to the provinces of Chihli (Hopei) and Shantung. The news from the north connected the disturbances with the Boxers, an organization of which neither the older missionaries nor the Chinese Christians had previous knowledge. The Boxers openly adopted the motto for their flag, "Protect the Empire; exterminate the foreigner." Toward autumn reports reached us that the Boxers had the backing of the Empress Dowager and that she had ordered to Peking (now called Peiping) Tung Fu-hsiang, the fierce and ruthless general who had quieted a Mohammedan rebellion in the northwest. It was reported that he had promised, in an audience with the Empress Dowager, to drive every foreigner out of China into the sea.

The *North China Daily News*, the authoritative newspaper of the resident English population, had been warning its readers since the *coup d'état* by the Empress Dowager in August, 1898, that there was a crisis in the north. Early in the spring of 1900 it called upon the diplomatic representatives of foreign countries to take definite steps to deal with the agitation against foreigners, and prophesied that unless this were done the whole country from the Yellow River to the Great Wall would soon be in a blaze of insurrection which would force every foreigner out of the Empire.

Some weeks before this the American, British, French, German, and Italian ministers had united in a request that an imperial decree be issued demanding the suppression of the Boxer organization. From that time until June the ministers of all the great powers were writing separate, or identical notes to the Chinese government. They were, as a body, demanding meetings with the *Tsungli Yamen* (the Chinese Foreign Office) or were meeting separately with individual members of the *Tsungli Yamen*. Finally they warned the *Tsungli Yamen* that it would be necessary to call upon the foreign navies unless the threats to foreigners ceased. All these efforts were futile either in halting the widespread riots and persecutions against foreigners and Chinese Christians, or in bringing from the throne any serious effort to insure protection. Thus it became clear that, with the Emperor and his corps of Chinese lieutenants out of the way, the Empress Dowager and the whole reactionary Manchu régime were lending their support to the Boxers.

In spite of all these indications of trouble, the missionaries in Nanking were making plans for their work as usual. At least twenty-five of them had spent a number of years in China, but their ears were strangely closed to the repeated warnings. As the summer approached their families proceeded to Kuling, a summer resort in the mountains near Kiukiang, a river port located about four hundred miles up the Yangtze River; they were apparently unconscious of the fact that if the general unrest over Manchuria, Mongolia, Chihli, Kansu, and Shantung should extend south to the Yangtze River, Kuling would be a trap for missionaries and other foreigners summering there.

Moreover, this was the year for the triennial examinations in Nanking. Not less than one hundred and fifty thousand visitors were expected in the city during the summer. The whole community was preparing to welcome the honored guests. Here was a unique opportunity to render service to this great gathering of scholars. A group of us in Nanking, with the coöperation of Dr. Timothy Richard, secretary of the Society for the Diffusion of Christian and General Knowledge among the Chinese, were planning for the distribution of literature among the scholars and arranging a series of lectures for them.

Early in May our plans had to be suddenly abandoned. Because of the disturbed conditions, an edict was issued from Peking canceling all examinations throughout the country. Although a great disappointment to me, even this did not serve as a warning of the impending peril. My family had already gone to Kuling with friends. With our plans changed, I left Nanking at once to join them and in order that I might continue language study during the summer, took with me Chia *Sien Seng* who had succeeded Mr. Ma as my teacher.

During the early days of June disturbing news began to come from Peking. The Government controlled the telegraph system, so the reports were brief and often garbled. Finally word leaked through that the foreign ministers in Peking were under siege, together with all other foreigners in that city as well as in Tientsin, and that we might expect to learn of their death at any moment. Our American minister and the ministers of all other countries were locked up in the British Legation in Peking, and were unable to communicate with their nationals throughout China.

After weeks of uncertainty a messenger came to our bungalow about midnight with a message from the British consul at Kiukiang, advising us to flee at once, as the Empress Dowager had ordered off the heads of all foreigners in China. Our servants were fully alive to the peril of the situation and did everything possible to help us get down at once to Kiukiang, where a Shanghai steamer was due the next day. At the suggestion of Teh-pao, our faithful and efficient cook, we dressed our children in Chinese clothes and the nurse took them in her sedan chair with curtains closely drawn, as a Chinese woman would travel. Mrs. Brockman rode in another chair. Teh-pao and I walked beside them. We hastened down the mountain and across the plain, a trip of fourteen miles, reaching Kiukiang just in time to catch the down-river steamer for Nanking.

The officers on the boat had brought news from Shanghai. It seemed clear that the Empress Dowager, a very tigress when aroused, would stop at nothing which her anger prompted. She was forceful and alert and had the backing of the Manchu reactionaries who had caused the overthrow of the Emperor. Would the officials of the Yangtze Valley and of the South obey the Empress Dowager's orders? The lives of several thousand foreigners hung upon the answer to that question. As the news from North China indicated, this would involve the Chinese Christians as well as the foreigners. There was some hope, however, in the statement given out by the British consul that Yüan Shih-k'ai, Viceroy of Shantung Province, Chang Chih-tung at Hankow, and Liu Kun-yi at Nanking, had agreed to disregard the instructions of the Empress Dowager.

On reaching Nanking we learned that Viceroy Liu Kun-yi had announced his determination to protect the foreigners. From my knowledge of him during the year and a half of residence in Nanking I was not surprised at his attitude, but I questioned his ability to control the fierce Hunanese troops, his only force for keeping order. Every day during the first week after our return, from one to four soldiers were beheaded because of their agitation against foreigners. Liu Kun-yi sent word to the missionary families still in Nanking, asking for their coöperation in avoiding trouble. There were to be no gatherings of Christians, no bright lights in our homes at night. He asked us not to leave our compounds after dark, and not to go at any time down into the business section of the city. He picketed our compound with guards carrying loaded rifles. Night and day we heard their tramp outside our house, which was only a few feet from the street. It was a question whether our guards were a protection or a menace, since no one knew at what moment they might revolt.

Very soon a placard was put on our front gate

giving warning that all foreigners in Nanking were to be killed on a certain night. When that night arrived, Mrs. Brockman and I took our two little children into the bedroom with us and, leaving a dim light burning, we attempted to sleep. About two o'clock in the morning I found myself standing at the foot of the bed. I had been aroused by two gunshots under our bedroom window and had jumped up before I was fully awake. I have never thought so rapidly nor so profoundly as I did on that occasion.

My conscience challenged me: Why have you done this? Why have you brought your wife and two little children into what may be worse than death? It is all right for you to have risked your own life, but what right did you have to do this?

The answer flashed into my mind: Because the Bible says, "Go ye into all the world and preach the Gospel to every creature."

Again my conscience spoke: The Bible says it. That's a book. The words may belong there, or they may not. It may be a mistake that they are in the Bible. But there is no doubt about your relation to your wife and children. You are responsible for them. Why did you do it?

I lived a lifetime within a moment, it seemed to me. And then the message came to me: No, not a book, I sent you. Be not afraid.

I did not question then, and have never since questioned, the validity or the source of this assurance.

I must make clear that there was no assurance against murder or experiences worse than murder. There was only the assurance that we were in the right place.

Teh-pao hurried into our room. "It is not an assault," he said. "The Hunanese Guard knew that the house had been posted, so they have fired off their guns to give you peace of mind and let you know that they are doing their duty."

A few days later the American consul insisted that all Americans leave Nanking, as he could no longer be responsible for their safety. Acting upon his advice, we hurriedly packed the necessary clothes and left with other refugees for Japan, where at Nikko we were surrounded by natural and artificial beauty equaled in few other spots on the earth. Fortunately, Mr. Ransford S. Miller of the American Legation was spending the summer in Nikko, and he and his family showed us all possible kindness. During our entire time in Japan, also, the Japanese were most considerate.

In spite of these favoring conditions, life was more difficult than in Nanking. More than fifty days had passed without news from those imprisoned in Peking. Among our fellow refugees were the wives of some of these men. The women had abandoned hope and were wearing mourning for their husbands. We dreaded to read the morning papers, fearing to find details of a horrible massacre of all Chinese Christians and foreigners in Peking. There was likewise but scant news concerning missionaries in many parts of the country who had fled from their homes in the troubled area in an attempt to reach the coast.

Finally, on the 9th of August, 1900, the news was flashed around the world that the allied forces had reached Peking, the legations had been relieved, and the foreigners and Chinese Christians rescued.

The precipitate flight of the Empress Dowager from the capital marked the collapse of her mad attempt to fight the whole world and to kill every Christian in China. But China would be long in paying the cost of her folly. As a tool of her madness the Empress had used the flaming patriotism of the humble and ignorant. The conflagration of ill-will and misunderstanding had spread throughout the Empire and could not be extinguished immediately. The treatment of foreign residents and Chinese Christians, both Protestant and Roman Catholic, had shocked the world.

This situation postponed the opening of my work in Nanking. On my return there in the autumn of 1900 I gave myself again to language study. The educational institutions had opened, but with a limited enrollment. Although the Yangtze Valley had escaped any serious outbreak, the situation was greatly changed. No missionary work was possible for the time being among non-Christians. Life in Nanking was quite different from that of only a few months before, but it afforded a favorable opportunity to study the Chinese people in the self-revela-

tion of the emotional shock incident to the outburst
of the Boxers. These days, however, marked the
nearest approach to utter discouragement that I ever
experienced. The Boxer outbreak had subsided, but
it had left among all the Chinese, except the Christians, a deep resentment against the foreign powers
and against all foreigners in China.

I had been sent out to work among the literati, or
the scholar class. Very few of them had accepted
Christianity since the arrival of Robert Morrison,
the first Protestant missionary, almost a hundred
years before. They were the element in the country
which best understood and most resented the im-
perialistic designs of the Western powers, and saw
most clearly the danger to China's most cherished
institutions. The approach to them, which seemed
difficult enough when I first arrived in Nanking, appeared almost hopeless after the Boxer upheaval.

As a boy I had visited Stone Mountain in Georgia,
a sheer precipice rising seven hundred feet from the
plain. I now pictured myself at the foot of this great
monolith drilling a hole with a pin and attempting
to blast the mountain. My work for the literati
seemed equally impossible.

Chapter V: Beyond the Flying Rainbow Bridge

By the end of 1900 I was beginning to explore the classics and was becoming interested in Chinese history and culture. After working at our books until the middle of the afternoon, Mr. Chia would take me, two or three times a week, into the city. Often we would visit in a teahouse, where he would introduce me to his friends and let me try out my language on them. On other days we would visit places of historic interest.

Every scholar in the nation was proud of Nanking even though its ancient splendor had departed. More than five hundred years earlier the second emperor of the Mings had transferred the court to Peking, and only thirty years previously the Taipings had withdrawn, leaving Nanking in ruins. Where once had stood the imperial palaces we now saw a farmer plowing with his water buffalo.

Mr. Chia would frequently entertain me with stories of the grandeur of Nanking's past. One of the most famous bits of Nanking's glory was the Porcelain Tower. One afternoon we went to the place where it had stood, and for a few cents purchased from an antique-dealer a porcelain brick which had been taken from the ruins of this structure. Here is a description of the Tower written by a Dutch traveler in 1665, a member of the second Dutch embassy to the Emperor of China:

"In the middle of the Plain, to which they ascended by twelve steps, stands a high Tower of Porcelain, which for costliness and all manner of rare workmanship, hath not its parallel in all China. It consists in nine vaulted stories, to be ascended on the inside by a hundred and four steps. Round about every story is a Gallery curiously adorn'd with Images and Windows; on both sides of which are square Holes for the Light to come in at, with Ivory Bars; all the Work on the outside Polish'd or Glaz'd with divers colours, as Red, Green, and Yellow: The whole structure made of several Pieces so curiously cemented together, that it seems to be one entire thing. Between the Galleries are Juttings out, made like Penthouses, and colourr'd with Green; at each corner whereof hang small Copper Bells, which mov'd by the wind make a continuous and pleasant tinkling. The upper part of the Tower, to which none can get, unless they climb up the outside, is Crown'd, as the Chinese say, with a great Pine-apple of Massy Gold from which upper Gallery they may see, not only over the whole city of Nanking, but all the adjacent Plains, as far as the Eye can reach."[1]

[1] John Nieuhoff, Steward to the Embassadors. *The Embassy of Peter DeGoyer and Jacob DeKeyzer from the Dutch East India Company to the Emperor of China in 1655* (translated from the Dutch), p. 287.

I mention such excursions as this with my teacher because they did much to build a consciousness of the background of Chinese civilization.

As I was preparing for work in behalf of the literati, the place of greatest interest to me in the city was the Examination Hall. At this time the old educational system of China was still in force. It had lasted, almost unchanged, for two thousand years. It is true that through the influence of Li Hung-chang, naval and military academies had been established recently at Tientsin, Nanking and Foochow, as well as a modern mechanical and engineering college at Tientsin. But these institutions exerted no influence upon the ancient educational system of the government which tested students by examinations held at prefectural centers. To the most proficient it granted the *Hsiu Ts'ai*, or Budding Genius, degree, which foreigners have roughly translated Bachelor of Arts.

In the viceregal centers once each three years those who had taken this first degree were qualified to stand for the *Chü Jên*, or Man of Distinction, degree, which has been called the equivalent of Master of Arts, although it was much more difficult to attain than our Doctor of Philosophy. Sometimes scholars took the examination every three years unsuccessfully until they were sixty years of age. Out of the total number taking the examination only about one-half of one per cent were awarded degrees. At the vice-regal capitals permanent equipment was provided for the examination of the candidates for the Man of Distinction degree.

Triennially there was held in Peking a special examination at which those who had secured the Man of Distinction degree could compete for the *Chin Shih*, or Doctorate. As in the case of the other examinations, degrees were conferred upon but a limited number.

The number of scholars who took the examinations at Nanking was much larger than at any other provincial capital. While Canton, Tientsin, and other centers had something like ten thousand scholars, Nanking had provision for about thirty thousand. Nanking was proud of its scholastic preëminence among the provincial capitals. The city not only had a larger number of applicants for degrees, but furnished more than its share of the most eminent scholars of the nation. Mr. Chia told me with evident pride of the large number of Nanking men who had won a place in the famous Hanlin Academy at Peking, a very distinguished honor. With even greater pride he explained to me that during the past sixty years twenty-six men had been given the distinction of Highest Scholar in the Empire, and of these, seventeen had taken their degrees at Nanking, and four were then living in the city. The local organization of the literati in Nanking was the most influential in the country.

I was eager to see the Examination Hall, and amazed when I did see it. Surrounded by a wall twenty or more feet high, it covered several blocks in the heart of the city. The wall was unbroken except on the south side, where a massive gateway lifted its stately form. Three turnstiles, called "West," "East" and "Middle," were provided in this Great South Gate. Entering there, Mr. Chia and I faced a central avenue which ran northward, bisecting the grounds. As we walked along we saw thousands of cells or stalls in rows running east and west at right angles to the avenue. There were one hundred and twenty cells in each row, all facing south on a narrow passageway. Within these cells, Mr. Chia told me, scholars were confined during the three assignments in the examination period, each one of which required from thirty-six to seventy-two hours, according to the ability of the scholar. During this grilling test the door of each cell was locked and sealed.

I was told there were nearly thirty thousand of these cells built of brick and covered with gray tiles. Each cell was four feet wide, four feet deep and six feet high. High up at the back of the cell was the only storage space it contained, a narrow shelf. Below was the scholar's seat, another narrow shelf about eighteen inches from the ground. A wooden plank was provided which served as a writing-table when placed on narrow projecting ledges on opposite walls of the cell. In addition to these simple furnishings, each scholar was given a candle, some paper, a slab of ink and a set of camel's-hair brushes. His food and other necessities were passed to him by an attendant through a lattice in the door.

In the center of the great enclosure was a watch-tower some sixty feet in height which commanded a view of the entire area. There were five smaller towers in other parts of the enclosure. Officials stationed in these during the period of the examinations were on watch night and day to see that nothing was done contrary to the regulations.

Before the examinations were formally opened, the leading officers gathered in the great central tower, and from there were distributed the subjects for the essays. Mr. Chia told me that from this moment a stillness like that of the great deep rested over the broad expanse of the Examination Hall. I pictured in my mind the scene, with tens of thousands of brushes limning the strange hieroglyphics. Each man, like his own angel of judgment, wrote his own life sentence. No other nation has ever devised such an intellectual test; the scholars of no other nation could or would endure such an ordeal. From among the twenty-eight thousand or more contestants only about one hundred and forty men could get the coveted Man of Distinction degree. When the results of the examination were determined the names of the successful scholars were written on the Lion-Tiger Board outside the Great South Gate.

When we reached the far end of the avenue we faced the entrance to the official headquarters. This was a huge place, for it housed the chief examiner and his assistants during the period of the examinations, a month or six weeks. A low wall divided the headquarters from the section occupied by the scholars. Mr. Chia explained that in addition to the chief examiner and his staff, who came with him from Peking, many distinguished scholars from all parts of the viceroyalty were brought in to assist in the reading of the papers. There were also thousands of copyists, for every essay had to be copied before it came to the attention of the examiners.

Within this section was a space cut off from the rest of the headquarters by a canal and spanned by the Flying Rainbow Bridge. All the essays were given a preliminary reading, and the best ones were then sent across the Flying Rainbow Bridge, where eminent scholars gave final judgment in the selection of the small number which would win for their authors the Man of Distinction degree.

I stood for some time in front of the Flying Rainbow Bridge, meditating on this educational system. The Man of Distinction degree was required for entrance into official life. Any man, however poor or humble, had the same opportunity to take the examinations and win the degree as had his wealthy and influential neighbor. The thought came to me that beyond the Flying Rainbow Bridge was the mind of China—and not only the mind but the conscience also, for the primary characteristic of the required learning was *moral*. No man could assume control over the government of the Chinese people or sit in judgment on their affairs whose mastery of the principles of China's moral heritage had not been proven. Here was a system of selecting rulers, which China had devised and carried on, in somewhat varied form but without serious interruption, for two thousand years. Granted that the experiment of twenty centuries had not been entirely satisfactory, because no written examination can be proof of man's moral character, was not this old system of selection one of the noblest experiments of all human history? Although I was but half conscious of the fact at the time, I soon began to take a pride in Nanking's scholastic record. And as I learned more and more about the literati, I became slowly and involuntarily impressed with this educational system which had so long held the loyalty and confidence of the whole nation.

My reading of the *Sacred Edict* had caused me to ask myself questions which, then, I did not try to answer: to that point I had lost nothing from my store of home-grown preconceptions of Western superiority. While I had begun to raise questions about the good in China's civilization, I must make it clear that this was only the dawn of my changing attitude: from a critical hunting out of the bad to a just appreciation of the good which I found in China, was a long slow process. It was not until I visited Peking after the Boxer Rebellion that my sense of western superiority became shaken: only then did I begin to feel that we foreigners had much to learn from China.

Chapter VI: The Martyrs and the "Armies of the Lord"

I MADE an extended visit to Peking in the summer of 1901 with my colleague, Robert R. Gailey of Tientsin. We were there on the first anniversary of the relief of the legations. As I reflected upon this experience, it impressed me deeply and came to have a distinct bearing on my conception of the relation between Western and Oriental cultures.

The Imperial Court had not yet returned from Shensi Province, to which it had fled upon the entry of the allied troops. The palace buildings were still parceled out among the armies of Europe, America, and Japan. Through the courtesy of its guardians, Gailey and I were given permission to visit the private apartments of the Emperor. Here were the model railway, the telephone and telegraph instruments, clocks and other contributions of science to modern civilization, with which he had amused and educated himself as a youth. We visited the Throne Room of the palace and saw the Golden Dragon Throne from which he had issued the memorable reform edicts, prepared by his coterie of patriotic and brilliant young reformers at the cost of their lives or of banishment from China.

As we stood near the throne upon which the Emperor had sat as the ruler of a third of the population of the world, I pictured him in all the magnificence which had surrounded him. A young man, almost exactly my own age, he was allowed to rule his people for but a few brief days.

Finally, we came to the prison in which the Emperor had been confined. It was located on a small island in a lotus lake. The walls of his study were filled from floor to ceiling with quotations from the classics written in large and beautiful characters. I saw the complete file, left in the hurry of his departure, of *The International Review of the Times* (*Wan Kuo Kong Bao*), the magazine published by the Society for the Diffusion of Christian and General Knowledge among the Chinese, and edited by my old friend, Dr. Young J. Allen. We saw hanging on the wall all that a vandal souvenir-hunter had left of the beautiful clock which marked the slowly moving hours of the Emperor's imprisonment. My heart went out strangely to him. I had a great longing to know him personally, for he had revealed certain characteristics which made a strong appeal to me. He saw clearly the condition of his country; he moved with dispatch to correct the evils; his courage was dauntless, his devotion unsurpassed. He gathered about him instinctively the noblest and ablest men, Chinese despised by the Manchu lords. Would he yet come back to power and, surrounded by the survivors of the group of young reformers, lead his country into a new and glorious future? Would God thus make the wrath of man to praise him? I felt myself in the midst of mighty unseen forces.

My first visit to these places associated with the Emperor turned my thoughts to the reformers with whom his destiny was so intimately associated. For these reformers Dr. Timothy Richard's writings were one of their main sources of inspiration. He had been called into their inner councils, and at their suggestion had been asked to become adviser to the Emperor. I later sought out Doctor Richard and asked him about his experience with the reformers, his estimate of their leaders, and his appraisal of their program. I find that I still have a journal giving an account of my interview with him, in which he sketched at some length the character and attainments of these unfortunate patriots; and those notes now corroborate my recollection of that conference.

The outstanding leaders among these reformers, he told me, were K'ang Yu-wei, T'an Tsu-t'en and Liang Ch'i-ch'ao. K'ang, the oldest, had taken his *Chin Shih* (Doctor's degree) some years before at Canton and was famous because of his commentary on the Chinese classics. In this work he had announced his conclusion that Chu Hsi, whose commentaries for several hundred years theretofore had been considered authoritative, had been wrong in defining Heaven as law instead of as God, and thus had misled China as to the personality of God.

T'an, although much younger, was recognized

among the reformers as their leader. His father was the Governor of Hupei and his mother, it is interesting to note, was a Christian. T'an had a strong face that bore testimony to the earnestness of his spirit. Among these men he was the statesman, as K'ang was the scholar.

Liang was youngest of the three and the most brilliant. He had taken his *Chü Jên* (Master's degree) at Canton when only twenty-three years old. To him Doctor Richard referred as the fastest talker, quickest thinker, and clearest writer he ever knew—a judgment which I later came whole-heartedly to indorse.

These were only a few of the several men whom the Emperor summoned to his aid, but their characters and attainments are typical of the rest of that brave and far-sighted band who stood by him to the end. I will give Doctor Richard's own words in his account of the dethronement of the Emperor and the death of the reformers:

"I never saw the Emperor. The very hour of my first audience with him as his adviser had been the time fixed by the Empress Dowager to take over the government. There was great excitement among the reformers. T'an called upon me, much agitated, and Liang informed me that the Emperor's life was in danger. All gates to Peking were closed. The heads of the reformers were ordered off. I was bound to do the best I could to save these men. I took the first train for Tientsin and hastened to the British Consulate to intercept the British minister on his way from the summer resort, Peitaiho, to Peking. I pleaded with him for an hour, explaining to him that the reformers meant no harm, that they had done nothing but support their own Emperor, and had committed no crime. I might as well have pleaded with a stone wall.

"K'ang and Liang escaped to Tientsin, where they boarded a boat bound for Shanghai. They besought T'an to accompany them, but he refused because he had not reported to the Emperor concerning a commission in Tientsin with which he had been intrusted. His high sense of honor made him insist upon returning to Peking, although he realized that it could not affect the turn of events and that it meant certain death.

"The next day T'an and five of his colleagues were beheaded in the Vegetable Market Place in Peking, the common execution-ground. T'an awaited the executioner's ax with head bared, kneeling in an attitude of worship. When ordered to keep silent, he cried out:

"'You kill us, but for everyone that perishes today a thousand will rise up to carry on the work of reform and uphold loyalty against usurpation.'"

Such, I learned, were the men who suffered martyrdom for their country. With reference to the program of the reformers, Doctor Richard pronounced the ninety and more edicts issued during those few months by the Emperor as "brilliant, none more brilliant in the history of the world."

Gailey and I spent several days viewing the complete destruction of the different mission stations in which had been located the residences of the missionaries, the hospitals, schools, and in some cases the colleges.

We first made the round of the Protestant mission stations—the London Missionary Society, the Church of England, the American Board, the Presbyterian and the Methodist. All were in utter desolation. The buildings had been burned, and even their foundations dug up and carried away. Nothing remained of the Methodist mission, which had covered several city blocks near the Legation Quarter, except a charred wall that stood as a monument to the destruction.

We then visited the Catholic stations. Catholic missionary work had been carried on continuously for more than three centuries, and in the four sections of the city imposing cathedrals had been erected. The East, West, and South Cathedrals had been destroyed. The Christians assembled in the South and East Cathedrals at the time of the outbreak had been slain. From the West Cathedral the priests and sisters and some of the Chinese Christians had been brought into the legations by a rescue party; others were massacred, and some thrown back into the burning building.

Near the West Wall of the city the North Cathedral was still standing, though severely battered. This cathedral had withstood a siege of sixty-two days, including twenty-eight successive days of continuous shelling. It had harbored, under the leadership of Bishop Favier, over three thousand Chinese Christians and thirty-two missionaries. During the entire period it had been defended by forty marines from the Legation Quarter whom the French and Italian governments had sent to the aid of the besieged.

The pilgrimage to these scenes of desolation and destruction was almost overwhelmingly depressing. A year had passed since the relief of the legations, but no attempt had been made to restore any of the waste places. Utter ruin still marked the wide track of the Boxers' madness. Our evenings were usually spent as the guests of various missionary families living in rented houses near the ruins of their mission compounds, and on these occasions the conversation consisted largely of stories of the heroic deaths of pastors, teachers, or Bible women. Here in Peking, Gailey and I saw the trail of devastation, but we reminded ourselves that it had spread widely over North China, through Mongolia and Manchuria and west to the borders of Burma, with a death toll certainly exceeding thirty thousand. When could the

Christian Church ever recover from what it had
suffered? It seemed folly to speak of the martyrs as
the seed of the Church.

The devastation caused by the Boxers had been
terrible, but the atrocities committed by the armies of
occupation far surpassed in barbarism the deeds of
the Boxers. The looting began from the very day
that the allied troops reached Peking for the relief
of the legations. Here is a picture given by an eye-
witness whom I met in Peking:

"That same night, very late, a transport corps
. . . came in hauling a multitude of little carts; and
within a few minutes these men were offering for sale
hundreds of rolls of splendid silks which they had
gathered on their way through the city. You could
get them for nothing. Some one who had some gold
in his pocket got an enormous mass for a hundred
francs. The next day he was offered ten times the
amount he had paid. In the dark he had purchased
priceless fabrics from the Hangchow looms which
fetch anything in Europe. . . . Everybody had
things for sale. We heard, then, that everything had
been looted by the troops from the sea right up to
Peking; that all the men had got badly out of hand
in the Tientsin native city, which had been picked
as clean as a bone; and that hundreds of terrible
outrages had come to light. Every village on the line
of march from Tientsin had been treated in the same

way. Perhaps it was because there had been so little fighting that there had been so much looting."[1]

The looting was not confined entirely to the soldiers. Under the protection of their occupation, civilians joined in the sack of the city. The eye-witness referred to above gives the story of how he spent the day following the relief of the legations. Here is the way his day began:

"I shall never forget the renewed sense of freedom when I went out the next morning with my men and some others. . . . Not a soul afoot, not a door ajar, not a dog. Nothing. It might have been a city of the dead. After all the roar of rifle and cannon which had dulled the hearing of one's ears for so many days there was something awesome, unearthly, and disconcerting in this terrified silence. What had happened to all the inhabitants?

"I had ridden forward slowly for a quarter of an hour or so, glancing keenly at the barred entrances which frowned on the great street, when suddenly I missed my men. . . . I rode back, rather alarmed, and shouting lustily. . . . Then suddenly, as I looked, there were several rifle-shots, a scuffle and some shouting, and as I galloped back in a sweat of apprehension I saw one of my men emerge from the huge *porte-cochère* of a native inn, mounted on a black mule. My men were coolly at work. They were providing themselves with a necessary convenience

[1] B. L. Putnam Weale, ed., *Indiscreet Letters from Peking*, p. 328. Dodd, Mead & Co., New York, 1906.

for moving about freely over the immense distances. In the courtyard of the inn two dead men lay, one with his head half blown off, the second with a gaping wound in his chest. My remaining servants were harnessing mules to carts, and each, in addition, had a pony ready saddled to receive him, tied to an iron ring in the wall. I angrily questioned them about the shots, and pointed to the ghastly remains on the ground; but they, nothing abashed, as angrily answered me, saying that the men had resisted and had to be killed. . . . Then in a body we sallied forth, this time a fully-equipped and well-mounted body of marauders."[1]

A whole year was spent in the looting of Peking. As Gailey and I rode out to the Summer Palace, fifteen miles beyond the city, we passed a stream of carts belonging to one of the European powers. These were driven and guarded by soldiers in uniform and were piled high with loot gathered from the Summer Palace. Eight years later I found this loot of Peking being offered for sale at bargain prices in the great cities of Europe.

The curse of the foreign armies did not bear as heavily upon Peking as upon surrounding districts, because in Peking they kept something of a watch on one another. Dr. George Morrison, British adviser to the Chinese government and distinguished correspondent of the London *Times*, was in Peking at the time and told me that after the Boxer outbreak had

[1] *Ibid.*, pp. 329-332.

been completely suppressed one of the great European powers, without a shadow of excuse, had sent its soldiers over the lower part of the province, destroying village after village and committing atrocities upon innocent Chinese. This had been done for the distinct purpose of bringing about a counter-revolution which would afford this nation an excuse to occupy the province permanently. Doctor Morrison emphasized the point that the soldiers of this one European country alone had been guilty of more atrocities than the Boxers had committed throughout all of China, Manchuria, and Mongolia.

Two most trustworthy historians of the Boxer outbreak are Captain F. Brinkley of Yokohama and Dr. Arthur H. Smith of Peking. I give their appraisal of the conduct of the European armies of occupation. Captain Brinkley writes:

"The facts as to the campaign conducted by foreign forces during parts of 1900 and 1901 in Chihli (Hopei), are that robbery, assassinations, and nameless outrages were committed by some of the men; that numbers of innocent and peaceful noncombatants were slaughtered or stripped of everything they possessed; that expeditionary columns, sent against villages which had not been guilty of any offence, looted the residences of the chief local officials, and shot down many of the inhabitants, and that whole districts were ruthlessly and needlessly laid waste. The seeds of hatred sown in that evil time must add their quota to the crop of tares that overgrows so much of the story of foreign intercourse with China. Anglo-Saxons and Japanese took scarcely any share in the sowing, for which forbearance much credit accrued to the latter in Chinese eyes, whereas there was probably little discrimination in favour of the former."[1]

Like Doctor Morrison, Doctor Smith was among the besieged in the British Legation; moreover, he spent the ensuing year traveling far and wide over the whole province to secure as accurate information as possible. This gives added value to his words:

"Immediately after the siege was raised, Peking was divided among the armies of invasion for purposes of patrol and as a base for possible operations elsewhere. . . . For the remaining months, until the end of the year, there was an increasing series of military expeditions in every direction from Tientsin and from Peking, some of which were on a large scale and fully reported, while others attracted little attention. . . . The circumstances of the Boxer uprising appear to have convinced the commanders of the armies of invasion that the rules of international law had no application to China at that time. . . . There have been times when it has seemed as if the foreign troops had come to northern China for the express purpose of committing within the shortest time as many violations as possible of the Sixth, the

[1] F. Brinkley, *China, Its History, Arts and Literature,* vol. xii, pp. 214-215. Oriental Series, Author's Edition, J. B. Millett & Co., Boston and Tokyo.

Seventh, and the Eighth Commandments. The combined result has been such a state of chaos in many districts as is at once incredible and indescribable. Of the promiscuous murder of noncombatants there is overwhelming evidence, which need not be cited. . . . As the result of all that gloomy winter one of the lessons which have been impressed upon the Chinese in varied but convincing forms is the moral inferiority of foreigners to Chinese."[1]

What I saw during my stay in Peking corroborated Doctor Smith's words in no small measure, and I came to see more clearly the futility of military force as a way of life among nations.

For me the most impressive single event during my stay in Peking was a conference of the Christians of the province of Chihli, where there were present representatives of the remnant of the Christian Church. Among these Chinese Christians at the conference almost every one had lost some member of his family, and many bore on their own bodies the marks of their persecution. One man, whose neck and face on one side were horribly disfigured, had been thrown, supposedly a corpse, onto a heap of bodies to be cremated, and only the burning of his face had brought him back to consciousness.

A Christian from one of the near-by villages gave the story of a little boy. The Boxers had demanded

[1] Arthur H. Smith, *China in Convulsion*, vol. ii, pp. 713-718. Fleming H. Revell & Co., New York, 1901.

that he denounce Jesus Christ. When he refused, they threatened to cut out his tongue. His last words were a reiteration of loyalty to Christ, after which the threat was executed. The speaker described the boy as happy and even exultant. The story deeply touched and at the same time inspired the group.

At another session the delegates were asked to tell their plans for the coming year. Professor Chen Wei-ping of Peking University, a young man in his twenties with whom I had been intimately associated in student work, stood up and in a quiet voice said:

"A short time ago my father was sent as pastor to a heathen village in the southern part of the province. He and my mother had not been there long enough to gather together more than a few Christians. The Boxers came from another part of the province and aroused the non-Christian inhabitants. They murdered my father, mother, and beautiful sister. I had expected this next year to continue my work at the university, in which I am deeply interested. But now there is only one place to which I can go, and only one piece of work that I can do. I must go to serve the people in that village. I must call together those who killed my father, mother and sister. I must tell them that I love them and have come to serve them in the place of my father. I must go there."

That day's experience convinced me that something had been planted in China which could never die. It was something unutterably precious—this

young Church. I had gone to the conference greatly
discouraged, but that one meeting of Chinese Christians established my confidence in the work of missions as had no previous experience in my life. I now
came to see that the Christians furnished the apolo-
getic for Christianity; most of those who had endured persecution could not have given forceful
arguments to prove any of the Christian doctrines,
yet there they stood before us, bereaved and ruined,
but filled with no bitterness—only forgiveness and
love; and the little boy whose tongue had been cut out
spoke more convincingly with his silence than he
could have done with his voice. I thought back to
what I had seen—whole sections of the city burned to
ashes, villages laid waste, temples despoiled; these
had stirred in me a feeling of futility. But these
living persons before my eyes, individuals who had
suffered for their beliefs—not for their worldly goods
—this sight inspired me with an admiration and a
hope before the intensity of which all sense of futility
was prostrated. To me the essential thing became the
living of Christianity.

Chapter VII: The Most Worthy

As MY plans for work with the literati developed I found the difficulties were formidable, and consulted with the more experienced missionaries in Nanking. The literati seemed unified in their prejudice against Christianity, the foreigner, and everything which suggested a change in the immemorial past. Scattered all over the city and with no place of general assembly, they were difficult for me to reach. My advisers recommended that I secure a Chinese Christian colleague who was a Confucian scholar, that I rent a modest place in the center of the city, which should serve as an informal club where I could keep open house and provide occasional lectures; thus I would gradually learn what would attract the literati.

This program appealed to me but presented what seemed an insuperable obstacle. The International Committee in New York, under which I was serving, supplied no funds for such purposes, and the Christians in Nanking were not able to finance the undertaking. There were no prominent Chinese Christians in the city, and not one man of sufficient means to make a contribution of twenty-five dollars.

I decided to go to Shanghai and again consult Dr.

Timothy Richard. Arriving there, I made my way to his office. With the graciousness which he always showed, he was eager to learn of my affairs. I explained my difficulties and asked his advice as to how I should proceed.

"That is easy; just do what the Bible says."

"What does it say, Doctor Richard, about this situation?"

"Why, it says, 'Go to the most worthy.'"

"But there are no 'most worthy' in Nanking," I said. "They are all Confucianists, Buddhists, Taoists, or Mohammedans."

"The Bible doesn't say anything about Confucianists, Buddhists, Taoists, or Mohammedans. It says 'the most worthy,' and there are some 'most worthy' men in Nanking. In every city of China there are men who are honest, unselfish, and universally trusted. Go back to Nanking and hunt out these men; lay before them your desire to help the young men of the city. You will find that they are interested and that they will coöperate with you."

"Do you mean to say, Doctor Richard, that a Confucianist would contribute to Christian work?"

"Most certainly. If you let them know that you are trying to help the young men build nobler characters, they will not hesitate to coöperate with you, because it is Christian. I have repeatedly proved this in my own experience."

At the end of our brief conversation my mind was

in a whirl. Could it be that Dr. Timothy Richard had compromised with heathenism?—Doctor Richard, whom I had thought of as one of the most splendid Christians and greatest missionaries, a man whom every Chinese, educated and uneducated, seemed to know and revere, and whose books were read all over the country by the literati? Had he lost the true conception of Christianity?

The shock left me stunned. I returned to Nanking in greater perplexity than when I had left. Although I saw no way to set up my work, I was determined not to enter into an alliance with heathenism. I was still loyal to my "Georgia swamp" theory of missionary work.

I continued to struggle, mentally and spiritually, with this disturbing problem, but circumstances soon changed my relation to it. I was appointed national secretary, with headquarters at Shanghai. In this capacity I was called before long to meet a financial emergency which had arisen in the Hongkong Young Men's Christian Association. There was one Christian of means in that city, Mr. Li, who had made an initial subscription of fifteen hundred dollars to launch the program. A few of the Chinese Christians had rented an upper room, gathered together a group of young men, organized an Association and elected a board of directors. Their budget showed that the money given by Mr. Li would carry them for a couple of months, but they would need an additional two thousand dollars to finance them through the year.

When I reached Hongkong I was informed that Mr. Li had suddenly lost all of his money. Moreover, there was no other Christian in Hongkong who could be expected to give more than a few dollars. The members of the board, young and inexperienced men, had the usual Chinese business caution and would not go ahead until they knew where they were coming out financially. A meeting was arranged at which I was to advise with them, and I was there with a set speech. I opened up the great possibilities of their work, called attention to the fundamental principles upon which it was founded, and described its success in other countries. Finally I referred to the financial needs. Making light of this difficulty, I assured the board that they should not worry about money. What they needed, I declared, was faith. The chairman, Mr. Tong Kai-son, with a manner alert, direct, decisive, stopped me to ask if I would mind an interruption.

"You tell us to have faith. You deal in faith. But we are business men. We have to pay our debts in dollars. If you could turn your faith into dollars, it would be all right."

I did some rapid and thorough searching of heart. He is right, I said to myself. Unconsciously I have been a hypocrite. I must be genuine.

"You are quite right, Mr. Tong," I replied. "If I cannot turn my faith into money, it is of no use.

I promise you that I will not leave Hongkong until we have the necessary funds to carry us through the rest of the year."

I had expected that the board would then discuss the matter and outline a plan of procedure. Instead, they adjourned at once and left the responsibility on my shoulders. Never have I faced a financial demand which seemed so impossible to meet. I turned to Southam, the local secretary who had arrived from Canada but a few months before to assume his responsibilities, a man of simple but profound faith. Neither of us could see any recourse but prayer. After an intense season of intercession we agreed that we would call on Mr. Li. When we laid the situation before him, he said:

"I have lost everything that I had. I am greatly interested in what you are doing and would gladly support it if I could."

"What other Christian is there," I asked, "among your friends to whom we could turn?"

"There is no other Christian in Hongkong who has any money," he replied. And then after a pause he said, "There is my brother. He is not a Christian and he doesn't live in Hongkong, but he is coming here on Thursday and I will be glad to take up the matter with him."

As we left his home we said that we should return Thursday. But I remarked to Southam: "No hope there. His brother is not a Christian, doesn't even live in Hongkong. What are we to do?"

"The only man that I can think of is Mr. Feng Hwa-chen."

"What! the famous Confucianist?"

"Yes. One of his clerks is in our evening classes, and through him Mr. Feng may have learned of what we are doing. He is probably the most influential Chinese in Hongkong and is highly respected for his moral character. He may help us."

I finally acceded to Southam's suggestion and he arranged an interview with Mr. Feng, who received us with formal courtesy. As I placed the situation of the young men's work before him I kept my eyes on the delicate features of his sensitive face, but they remained immobile.

"Have you the budget with you?" he asked.

I handed it to him. He read it attentively, then threw it on the desk with seeming disapproval. He turned to me and asked, "Do you mean to do all of that work with so little money?"

"Yes; the board has prepared the budget carefully."

His expression changed to one of cordial interest.

"You gentlemen have come across the Pacific Ocean to help our young men. You ought not to be tramping around the streets in this heat to raise money. You give your time; the least that we Chinese can do is to provide the funds. Leave this budget with me. I will take care of the expenses."

My first thought was that I had failed to make clear the Christian nature of the undertaking, and I determined to save my religion even if we lost the money.

"Mr. Feng, you understand, do you not, that this is a Christian institution and we teach the young men Christianity?"

"Yes, of course I do, but won't you let a Confucianist give to it?"

On Thursday, but with no hope of help from Mr. Li's brother, we called according to agreement. It was not until we had talked for some time that he said: "By the way, my brother has come back. I spoke to him about the work for young men and your financial problem, and he said that he would be glad to provide you with the money which you need."

Southam was able to call the board together and tell them that each dollar of faith had been turned into two dollars of Hongkong currency.

As I meditated upon the experience I could not doubt that God had led us. God had given us the money. Our faith had been honored. What I had to explain to myself was the fact that in answer to our prayer for funds, God had given them to us through two Confucianists. It had been done with no taint of compromise and with no possibility of misunderstanding. But Dr. Timothy Richard had earlier advised me to follow the same course in Nanking and I had been unwilling because it seemed a

sacrifice of principle. If God had led me in Hongkong, my course in Nanking must have been wrong.

Another incident which contributed to my education happened about the same time in Shanghai. Mr.
and Mrs. Joshua Levering of Baltimore were there
on a visit to China. It occurred to a few of us that
it would be helpful to have Mr. Levering meet with
a group of the leading Chinese of the city and speak
to them. This was an unprecedented step in several
respects. In the first place, the Chinese, except among
Christians, did not attend lectures or public addresses of any kind; it was their custom to meet in
informal groups for discussion and conversation.
Again, the relation between the Chinese leaders of
the community and the foreign merchants had been
confined almost exclusively to necessary business
transactions. Also, we wanted to have Mr. Levering
not only deliver a message of good will from the
business men of America to those of Shanghai, but
to say something of the responsibility of the business
community for the moral environment of its young
men. This might easily have been misinterpreted as
Christian propaganda, and resented, so we initiated
the undertaking with not a few misgivings.

An invitation was sent to a small and select list
of bankers and merchants. It was explained that
Mr. Levering was one of the leading citizens of Baltimore, that he was a banker, merchant, philanthropist,
and had been the Prohibition candidate for President

of the United States. Almost every man invited accepted.

Mr. Levering's background made it desirable to "coach" him on his talk to the merchants and bankers. He was new to China. He was chairman of the Southern Baptist Foreign Missionary Board and had taken a prominent part in the foreign work of the International Committee of the Y. M. C. A. We feared he might easily allow his religious interest to imperil our future relationships with these Confucian gentlemen among whom we were trying to establish our first contacts.

I called on Mr. Levering at his hotel and took great pains to show him the delicacy of the situation and warn him that the meeting was intended to furnish a point of contact, and not as an occasion for Christian propaganda. Mr. Levering thanked and reassured me.

When I reached the hall on the afternoon of the meeting I was surprised to find that a large number of the men had already arrived. Mr. Levering was evidently impressed with the audience of distinguished-looking men dressed in gorgeous silk gowns. In his address he reminded them of the bond of common experience that bound business men of all countries, and explained the problems business was facing in America. He then emphasized the responsibilities which business men owed to the community, especially in guarding the character of the young men. He described how Baltimore and other American cities were dealing with this problem. The audience was delighted. All was going well.

Then with the same ease and intimacy with which I had heard him talk to a group of friends in his own parlor, Mr. Levering spoke about Christianity and its influence. He told of the Church and Christian institutions such as colleges, Y. M. C. A.'s and hospitals, in which the business men of America were interested. In his enthusiasm Mr. Levering had forgotten my warning. He did almost everything that I had asked him not to do. I was greatly disturbed. If these important Chinese leaders should feel they had been tricked, the meeting would be a decided handicap instead of a help in our future dealings with them.

After the meeting they gathered around Mr. Levering, and to my amazement one after another expressed cordial appreciation of the speech. In their conversation with one another they were seemingly enthusiastic. I was still uneasy, for I could not learn the real situation from anyone but the Chinese members on the committee who had arranged for the meeting. When I did consult them, they assured me the enthusiasm of the audience was genuine and that the invited guests recognized the occasion as a unique and valuable experience.

My fears had proved wholly unfounded. No unfortunate reaction resulted from Mr. Levering's speech then or later; on the other hand, its influence for good was decided and lasting. Before long we had found a number of those present to be of the "most worthy."

In helping me to overcome my strange reluctance to go to the "most worthy," I owe to the Christian colleges in China a great debt. My relation to the Student Christian Movement early brought me into close touch with the students and faculties of these colleges. During my first two months in the country I had made a tour of the Christian educational institutions in central and southern China, and for ten years or more thereafter I frequently visited each of the missionary colleges in different sections of the country. These visits usually included conferences with faculty members and leaders of the Student Christian Movement, evangelistic meetings with students, organization of Bible classes, and personal interviews. I also met the students in the intimate contacts of summer conferences and national conventions. While studying the language at Nanking I had conducted voluntary Bible classes among the students of the Anglo-Chinese College, afterward to become Nanking University. Mrs. Brockman and I had kept open house for students and faculty members.

All of these contacts gave me an opportunity to study the relation of the missionary college to the non-Christian religions, and to make an appraisal of the effectiveness of the colleges in the spread of

Christianity. Thus these colleges were a formative factor in my conception of my task in China.

During my early days in China I had found that there were among missionaries two theories as to the place of education in the missionary enterprise: first, that the function of the missionary school was to train the sons and daughters of Christians, and that its purview should be the need of the Christians; and second, that the function of the missionary school was to train youth from both Christian and non-Christian homes, and that its scope should include the needs of the whole nation.

Out of these two theories there grew two kinds of missionary educational institutions. Those with the more restricted policy confined their students almost exclusively to the children of Christians, and trained their students primarily for the ministry or for teaching in mission schools. The teaching of English was discounted, because a knowledge of English opened opportunities for the students in business and tended to tempt them from carrying out the purpose of their training. These institutions were small and were supported almost entirely by funds from abroad.

The other kind of missionary school, called an Anglo-Chinese college, welcomed non-Christians and endeavored to provide an institution so Christian in spirit and method that it would exert a Christian influence upon all students. These colleges, which had the nation as a whole in mind, were usually located in the large cities; in response to the eager demand of young men, and later of young women, they made a special point of offering classes in English. The Anglo-Chinese institutions were much larger than the schools primarily for Christians, and were supported in increasingly larger degree by the Chinese community.

My first reaction to the situation was to favor the smaller schools. It was clear, I argued, that the presence of a large number of non-Christian students in the Anglo-Chinese colleges would lower the spiritual tone of the student body. Moreover, the graduates who acquired English would be tempted, by the higher salaries which business or government could offer, to turn aside from preaching or teaching.

My visits to the missionary institutions of both kinds led me to reverse my early judgment. I found in the Anglo-Chinese colleges that all students attended daily chapel exercises. I was impressed with the seeming lack of religious prejudice on the part of the Confucian students; they took part in all the voluntary Christian activities, such as Bible classes, Sunday School, and meetings of the Christian Association, to much the same extent as the non-Christian students in America, and were as responsive to the evangelistic appeal. Moreover, the Christians in Anglo-Chinese schools were more aggressive in their religious work than those in the smaller institutions —doubtless because they felt that they were under the scrutiny of non-Christians, and that they had work to do to win their non-Christian fellow students.

Later I came to know many of the fathers of these Confucian students. Every one I met manifested loyalty for the institution in which his son was being educated; particularly was he grateful for the high moral standard maintained by the institution. He was proud to call the missionary who was president of the college his friend. What impressed me most was that the Confucian patrons of the colleges, even though generous contributors to their support, had no desire to control them and made no objection to the Christian teaching. Later, when the freedom of these institutions was greatly circumscribed, it was not due in any degree to Confucian influence, but to the propaganda of Communism in its effort to discount the influence of Christianity.

The Anglo-Chinese colleges have grown into, or united to form, eleven Christian universities located in strategic centers throughout the country. Their benefit to China is appreciated by Christian and Confucianist alike. My contacts with them showed me the wisdom of their policy of discovering a vital need in the Chinese community, of inaugurating practical measures to meet it, and, most important of all, of relying confidently for support of a good work upon the Confucian community where those who were "most worthy" were always to be found.

Chapter VIII: TheEast and the West in the Great Cities

It soon became clear to me that many of the more thoughtful Chinese were alarmed at the moral conditions in the large port cities such as Canton, Shanghai, and Tientsin, where the commingling of East and West was breaking down the safeguards to character and multiplying the allurements of vice in both civilizations. In fact, the reluctance on the part of the Chinese merchants to remove restrictions to foreign trade was often due to this fear of the disintegrating influence of the foreigner upon the moral life of the community. In such cases the leaders in the Chinese community understood full well that the position taken on this matter was to their financial disadvantage. When it became clear to them that the tide of modern commerce could not be turned back, they welcomed any practical suggestion as how best to meet the moral hazards which the new era involved.

The situation raised the question whether it were not possible to form a working arrangement between Christians and Confucianists in an effort to meet the moral peril to the young men and boys in these great cities. To show how my work threw light on this question, I shall choose freely from my experience instances of effective coöperation in three typical cities.

I was invited to a conference with the officers of the Chamber of Commerce in a proud, cultured, and conservative city in the Yangtze Valley. The president of the Pawnbrokers' Guild, a leading citizen, was spokesman. "Until a few years ago," he began, "the life of our city flowed as peacefully as a river in the plains. The son followed the father in business, and the grandson the son, generation after generation, ten, fifteen, in some cases seventeen generations without a break in the succession. At night the young men were at home; they delighted in reading the classics."

His idyllic mood changed. He paused, and in a tone which indicated the ominous import of the event he declared: *"Then the railway came."*

This was followed by a more impressive pause which seemed to imply that further details were hardly necessary. "The railway station is located beyond the city wall near the East Gate. Near it has been built a hotel—a scandalous place. In the evening there are dances, wine, and imported women. Our sons, instead of spending the time quietly at home as we did, troop through the city gate to that hotel and they do not return until the early morning hours. When they come to work later in the day they are listless, their eyes are bloodshot. We cannot turn our business over to them. We have repeatedly considered this situation in meetings of the Chamber of Commerce. At first we thought of building a competitive hotel within the city to attract our young men, but after discussion we came to the conclusion that our hotel would succeed only as we included the objectionable features of the hotel outside the gate. In all of your travels have you ever come in touch with a similar situation? Can you show us how to save our young men?"

In reply I explained to them the somewhat similar problem which had confronted us in the United States and Canada in the migration from the farms to the city. I suggested that the new day made new demands upon their social and religious life. I called attention to the lack of facilities for recreation in the city. As they had detected a reluctance on the part of the young men to study the classics, I suggested that it might be well for the time being to encourage the study of subjects which would fit them to meet the demands of the modern day. I reminded them that their sons were no doubt dreaming of representing their great firms in London, Paris, and New York; probably they could be induced to study French, English, and modern business methods. I assured them that there was a strong sense of moral and spiritual need in the hearts of their young men, and that their restlessness was in part a sign of this need rather than a proof of their profligacy. I suggested that they coöperate with the Christians of the city by furnishing equipment and running expenses for a Christian Association. This, I believed, would successfully compete with the allurements of the hotel.

The president of the Pawnbrokers' Guild, a man of tremendous energy and force of character, was on his feet in an instant. In his enthusiasm his arms, clothed with the wide sleeves of the Chinese gown, were moving in the air like the arms of a Dutch windmill in a storm.

"That's what we want! That's what we want!" he cried out with eagerness. "Will you speak before the entire Chamber of Commerce tomorrow and tell the members what you have told us tonight?"

It was an impressive audience, composed of the leading men of the city, which gathered the next day. Every suggestion that I made was formally adopted. Plans were inaugurated at once for a canvass to secure funds for a modest building and the first year's expenses of the Christian Association.

In a little more than a year I returned to the city for the dedication of the building which they had erected in the meantime. It was an attractive structure with an auditorium that would hold more than a thousand. This was used at times as gymnasium, banqueting-hall, or a place for receptions. Baths, dining-hall, and even a roof garden were among its features. The building had cost more than double the amount I had suggested.

At the dedication every prominent person in the city was present. Congratulatory scrolls, sent by eminent scholars, officials, and members of the gentry,

were hung in the building as evidence of the good
will of the donors. The membership had reached over
eighteen hundred and already the organization had
become the most prominent and popular institution
of the city. The building was thronged with young
men and boys. The hotel was forgotten. I was informed that the head of the Educational Association, in inaugurating the campaign for the new
building, had reassured the literati by saying, "If
Confucius were living today he would ride in an auto-
mobile, have electric lights in his house, and belong
to the Young Men's Christian Association."

One of the younger literati, a Christian and a
member of a family which had been prominent in the
life of the city for many generations, became the
executive head of this undertaking and has continued
in the position until today. Under him the whole
enterprise has had a marked influence upon the moral
and religious life of the whole city.

The second illustration I take from Manchuria.
In response to an invitation from the missionaries
in Kirin, I made a visit to that city in 1914 to confer with the provisional board of directors which had
been organized to carry on work for young men and
boys. I had requested them not to arrange any public meetings, but to leave the time free for conferences with leaders. When I reached the railway
station, which was some distance from the city, I
found a large delegation of prominent men to meet

me, including Mr. Fu, a member of the Provisional
Parliament; these men had come to accompany me
on the long cold ride to the city.

In the late afternoon, while on the way to a meeting of the provisional board of directors, I was taken
past a lot two hundred and thirty-eight by six hundred feet. It fronted on the great boulevard leading
from the city to the railway station. It was near the
government schools of the city and within five minutes' walk of the center of the business section. This
lot, I was informed, had been granted outright by
the government to the board.

Before leaving the city I called upon the Governor
and the Commissioner of Foreign Affairs. Both assured me that their strength and influence were at
the disposal of the board for the development of this
Christian undertaking. One could not doubt the gen-
uineness of their interest. The Governor had been
intimately associated with the similar undertaking
in Tientsin. From evidence which I gathered it was
clear that the board could proceed with the assurance
that it had the backing not only of the city officials,
but of the literati and the gentry as well. The undertaking prospered and its history in Kirin down
through the years has abundantly justified the early
expectations of coöperation between the Christian
and Confucian communities.

My third illustration comes from Korea. During
my first years in the Far East, Korea, although

nominally independent, was culturally still a part of China; and my field included both countries. In response to an invitation from Dr. Horace Underwood, I visited Korea during 1901 to confer with him concerning work for young men in Seoul. He explained that a survey of conditions in the city had been made earlier by D. Willard Lyon and an appeal had been made to America for a trained secretary. He felt the time was ripe for a special effort in behalf of the Yangbans, who were the scholars and the aristocrats. Up to this time they had been largely untouched by Christian influence from which they had held aloof with pride and self-sufficiency. The recent war between China and Japan, however, had profoundly affected them, and Doctor Underwood felt that they would now welcome coöperation from the West in making adjustments to the new era. I was particularly interested in accepting this invitation because the only Oriental whom I had known intimately before I went to China was a Korean classmate at Vanderbilt, Yun Tchi Ho, who had since returned home.

Two years later I returned to Seoul at the invitation of Philip L. Gillett, a graduate of Yale, who had been chosen in response to the appeal for a trained worker, and had arrived in Seoul some months earlier. He wished my help in launching a Young Men's Christian Association. Mr. John Wanamaker had offered to give the headquarters building for this work for the Yangbans in Seoul, on condition that a

suitable site for the building were given by friends
in Korea. This seemed an impossible condition to
Mr. Gillett and me; to us the difficulties seemed in-
surmountable. I was a total stranger there; Mr. Gillett had had his time so filled with the study of the
language that he had made but few friends and ac-
quaintances. The case seemed even more hopeless because our best advisers deemed it unwise at this stage
to ask the Koreans for any gifts. I found that my
friend Yun was governor of a province so far away
from Seoul that we could not have the advantage
of his advice and help. A meeting was called of men
in the city who might be interested. Among those
present were Mr. E. V. Morgan, the American minister; Doctor McLeavy Brown, Commissioner of Customs; Doctor Takagi, a graduate of Johns Hopkins
University and the head of the Japanese bank; the
Japanese minister; the Chinese consul-general; two
representatives from the Russian Legation; the head
of the German Language School; and several other
educational leaders. No subscriptions were solicited
at that time, but the next morning Doctor Brown
headed the list with a gift of one thousand yen. Doctor Takagi voluntarily undertook the responsibility
of securing gifts from the Japanese. Mr. Gillett and
I called on the Chinese minister, who not only indicated his willingness to subscribe, but expressed the
hope that all of the Chinese would become members.

Within a few days seven thousand yen had been
subscribed, which enabled us to consider buying the

property. The only lot with sufficiently wide frontage on the main street, in the section which had been agreed upon as the ideal location for the building, was owned by Colonel Hyun Hung-taik, a famous hero in Korea, who had risked his life to save the Queen when her assassination had been attempted. He had been asked frequently to sell this property and had definitely declined to part with it. Doctor Underwood knew him well and agreed to approach him. Gillett and I went with Doctor Underwood when he made the call. On the way he said:

"Since we cannot go beyond ten thousand yen for the property, it will be better to ask Colonel Hyun to match Mr. Wanamaker's gift by giving the lot. This may induce him to sell it for ten thousand."

The Colonel received us with graciousness in his guest-hall. Quite the opposite of the big, brusque, daring military official I had expected to meet, he was modest, gentle, and rather small of stature. Doctor Underwood took some time to explain the enterprise which was being launched. According to our agreement, he told the Colonel of Mr. Wanamaker's conditional gift of a headquarters building. He went on to say that we had thought of the Colonel as the John Wanamaker of Seoul, and hoped he would like to match Mr. Wanamaker's gift of the building with his lot on the main street. As he was speaking in Korean I was unable to follow the conversation, but they were soon both talking eagerly. Finally Doctor

Underwood turned to Gillett and me, and said: "The Colonel will be glad to give the lot."

After we had bowed our thanks and were out of hearing I inquired, "What does this mean? Do we get it for five thousand?"

"No, it is an outright gift. And the fact that this gift has been made by the Colonel will mean a great deal for the success of our enterprise, for, next to Yun Tchi Ho, he is the idol of the young men of Korea."

Mr. Gillett and I had entered upon the canvass for seven thousand yen. At the close, our list totalled over fifty thousand yen, and included one thousand from the Emperor of Korea, twenty-five thousand from the Korean government, five thousand each from Colonel Hyun and the American minister, one thousand from the Chief Commissioner of Customs, and one thousand from Doctor Underwood.

While the new building was under construction the work was carried on in two native residences. This enabled Gillett to find out what features would prove most attractive to the Yangbans. On my next visit to Seoul about a year later, I was surprised to see a number of the young men at the temporary headquarters busily knitting. Indicating an attractive young man in the group, I asked Gillett who he was.

"He is the nephew of the Emperor," Gillett replied; "one of several princes who have joined us."

"I never heard of this Korean custom of knitting," I remarked.

"Well," he said, "you know that according to the old custom a Yangban was disgraced if he did anything with his hands. He hardly dared brush a speck from his coat lest he incur the disgrace of manual labor. But now they realize that they are entering the industrial era; the one thing above everything else they wish to do is to use their hands. They want to become carpenters, blacksmiths, photographers, printers. There is no trade that the most distinguished of them is not willing to learn. As soon as our Association was organized they insisted that I should teach them something. They supposed that I knew all the trades. I knew none. My sister had come out to spend a year with us, and when I was describing my predicament at the dinner table, she said, 'I could come down and teach them how to knit.' They are knitting scarfs for their wives."

This knitting was the only feature of an industrial department that they were able to inaugurate until it was possible to secure an expert in industrial training from the West.

Five years elapsed before the handsome headquarters building on the main street of the city was ready for dedication. Dr. Timothy Richard, Mr. S. K. Tsao, a leading Christian layman of Shanghai, and I were asked to attend from China. A delegation was also invited from Japan. The exercises continued for three days, on two of which there were services morning, afternoon, and evening. At all of these the new auditorium, seating about eight hundred, was crowded. The interest was so great that men were willing to stand for two and three hours. The meetings were so arranged that different audiences were present at each session.

At the final meeting there were seated on the platform about forty men whom the Association wished particularly to recognize. Yun Tchi Ho, my Vanderbilt friend and now the leading Christian of Korea, was chairman. To his right was the Resident General, Prince Ito, whom Dr. Timothy Richard called the greatest statesman of Asia. To the chairman's left was one of the Korean princes. Among others were the Prime Minister of Korea and practically every member of his Cabinet, Count Okuma of Japan, the Consuls of the different countries represented at Seoul, and the heads of the Christian missions, including the Fathers of the Greek Orthodox Church. The best elements of the complex life in Korea were represented and all were united in their support of the enterprise. Mr. Salmons, the American Consul, read a thrilling message from Mr. Wanamaker. Prince Ito, in a brief but most impressive message, indorsed the undertaking and pledged his coöperation. I could not understand what Yun Tchi Ho was saying in his speech which came at the end of the exercises, but it was easy to see that his audience was deeply stirred. As he was concluding his address a man arose in the audience and made a brief statement. He was followed by another, and another. I discovered that they had interrupted Yun in order to make subscriptions. This man gave five hundred yen, that one a thousand, another five hundred; one man offered the deed to a farm that yielded two hundred bushels of rice each year. Yun finally stopped the interruptions and announced that others could make their contributions privately.

As I looked upon this scene it was almost impossible for me to realize that scarcely six years had passed since our first conference in Doctor Underwood's study when we had discussed the possibility of undertaking this work in behalf of the Yangbans of the city. Doctor Underwood had prophesied then that in a few years' time there ought to be four hundred young men who would be united in the effort. The reality far surpassed his vision.

Upon this visit I was staying at the home of my brother who had been invited to become Mr. Gillett's associate. Just before we had arisen from the breakfast the morning following the dedication, the private secretary to Prince Ito called to say that the Prince wished to give a banquet in honor of the visiting delegates. When we reached his palace that evening we found all of the highest Japanese officials present, as well as the business and professional leaders connected with the movement. Before the banquet was concluded Prince Ito arose and gave an address of perhaps an hour's length. He had neither the manner nor the trappings of Oriental grandeur. Small of stature, gentle in manner, he spoke intimately and with evident sincerity. He told of the struggle which he had made in Japan for religious freedom, explained the reason for his deep sympathy with Christianity, and expressed his unalterable conviction that no civilization could be lasting that did not have a basis of sound morality. He emphasized the value of religion in creating this morality. Finally, speaking of the Christian Association whose inauguration we were celebrating, he said, "I look upon it as my co-worker in the regeneration of Korea."

After the banquet I happened to be standing near His Highness when Mr. Tsao came up to say good-by to him. The Prince said to him, "Go back to China and see that you have religious liberty. Tell your great officials that it must be."

This story shows how a Christian undertaking may make such an appeal that it secures the support of the different nationalities and religions in the Far East. Here were Chinese and Japanese, Russians, British, and Americans, all coöperating with the Koreans; more significantly, here were Confucianists, Buddhists, Shintoists and Taoists, all contributing their financial assistance and their influence to a distinctly Christian undertaking. One asks, "Did such a promising beginning meet expectations?" The enterprise has much more than met expectations. Over a period of a quarter of a century it has shared in leadership with all constructive social and religious elements of the city and through the years has exerted a continuous, vital, and transforming influence in the lives of thousands of new Christians.

Each of the three enterprises cited above was remarkable in its issue. In every case we had what at the outset seemed an impossible task; in every case unexpected aid came from strategic quarters. And thus it was throughout my years in the Orient, where instances could be multiplied many fold.

I asked myself why there should be the enthusiasm, the sudden interest to coöperate among so many diverse nationalities as in Seoul, for example; or why an organization such as the Chamber of Commerce in that city in the Yangtze Valley should officially place its prestige and united effort behind a Christian undertaking—an instance without parallel so far as I know in a Christian country. Whatever the complete answer to these questions, some things were clear: in every case there existed a deep sense of need; with the new day had come unprecedented moral perils to youth; and the men of the Orient, regardless of nationality or faith, believed that they had found in Christianity a force which was adequate to meet the situation.

Chapter IX: Science a Bridge of Understanding

My few months of experience in work for the literati at Nanking convinced me that I did not have the special training necessary to make the effort a success. I had taken a classical course in college, but the literati had never heard of Latin or Greek literature, history, or civilization. I was not far enough along in the Chinese classics to interest them in discussing their own literature. What I knew they did not care to learn; and what they wanted to know I was unable to teach. At that time they were not interested in Western education. One could speak of Harvard, Yale, Oxford, or Cambridge, and arouse no curiosity. They were hearing rumors of the wonders of modern science and, strangely enough, this was the one subject in which their interest was genuine. Few of them had ever seen a railway locomotive. They inquired whether the reported existence of such a monster were true. Were there any in America? How fast did they go? How much coal did they eat? Could I explain how messages were carried over the telegraph lines from Peking, Shanghai, and Hankow to Nanking? They had heard, although they were not sure that it was true, that there was a wire which carried the human voice long distances.

Here, I perceived, was a point of contact if I were but equipped to take advantage of it. I explained the situation to John Mott in a letter and urged him to send out a man with scientific training. The letter reached him in Chicago. In the elevator which was taking him to the street level he saw his friend, C. H. Robertson, Professor of Mechanical Engineering in Purdue University. As a student at Purdue, Robertson had made an excellent record in physics and had been prominent in student activities. He was captain of the track, baseball, and football teams, and head of the Student Christian Association. Mott knew him well, and with characteristic promptness and decision said, "There's my man!" He stopped Robertson at the foot of the elevator, handed him my letter, pressed the call upon him, and left it for Robertson to decide within a few days' time. Although it meant an entire change in his life plans, Robertson soon accepted the call. Within a few months he and his family were on their way to Nanking.

In the meantime I sought some way of meeting the longing of the literati to learn about modern science. I heard frequent mention of the special work for the literati which had been carried on for some years under the direction of Reverend J. S. Whiteright, an Englishman and principal of a theological college in Chingchoufu, a prefectural capital in

Shantung Province. I decided to visit Chingchoufu, meet him and study his work at first hand.

In those days it was quite an undertaking to go from the coast city of Tsingtao into the interior. The railway now carries one farther in one hour than a whole day's journey by the mule litter of that time. It was my first visit to the home province of Confucius and Mencius, and the hours on the mule litter and even the nights in the Chinese inn never became tiresome or monotonous. I found Mr. Whiteright to be a man of rare culture, imagination, versatility, and complete devotion. He was dressed in Chinese clothes and lived the life of the Chinese. His duties as principal of the theological college were enough to absorb any person's time. "As I studied missionary work throughout the province of Shantung," he explained to me, "I conceived the plan of changing the attitude of the literati toward Christianity by assisting them to gain some conception of modern Western civilization."

Alongside the campus he had built a courtyard, surrounded on all sides with attractive but modest buildings. A reading-room and two guest-rooms occupied the east side of the court, a museum the south, a science lecture-hall the west, and on the north was a chapel. This court was to serve as a place for the faculty and students of the theological college to meet with the people of the educated and official classes. The entrance to the court was through the museum. As I entered the museum I saw models of railways, electric cars, improved agricultural implements, and other products of modern science. A beautiful model of Westminster Abbey was on view; also models of other famous church buildings, hospitals, universities, and other institutions devoted to the uplift of man. There were diagrams and pictures skillfully prepared to dissipate superstition.

The lecture-hall, I learned, was used chiefly during the month when the prefectural examinations were held. Just as the capital cities like Nanking and Tientsin once every three years held examinations for the Man of Distinction degree, the prefectural capitals throughout the country held annual examinations for the Budding Genius degree. About ten thousand students, Mr. Whiteright informed me, came to Chingchoufu each year. During this time he provided two lectures a day. I will name a few of the twenty-nine lectures which had been given in April of that year: Steam Engines and Railways; Earthquakes and their Causes; Steamships and Navigation; Electric Telegraph; Methods of Western Education; History of the Origin of Buddhism; Advantages of Christianity to the Nation; What Methods Are Proposed by Western Engineers to Prevent Overflows of the Yellow River. He surprised me by saying that practically every student attended one or more of these lectures. While the lectures were inaugurated in behalf of the visiting students, Mr. Whiteright found that the demand for them continued all during the year. Groups of officials were particularly interested. A special series of lectures was given to the County Superintendents of Education in the district, at their request. Mr. Whiteright informed me that there would be no difficulty in greatly increasing the demand for lectures if he were able to provide them.

What astonished me most was to learn that during the month of the examinations preaching was carried on continuously in the chapel of the court from eight o'clock in the morning to six in the afternoon. Six men were required for the preaching and for interviewing those who wished to make personal inquiries concerning Christianity. The average attendance at the church services was one thousand. On Sunday the chapel was filled to overflowing even though the museum and science-hall were closed. A larger number attended the chapel services than the science lectures, and yet had there been no museum, no lectures, and no special approach to the students, very few could have been expected in the chapel services.

While visiting different cities of the province I made special inquiry as to the influence of Mr. Whiteright's work. Without exception the testimony was given that the attitude of the people toward Christianity throughout the province had shown a marked change as a result of this work in Chingchoufu. The results so far had been a diffusion of knowledge and the creation of an interest, rather than an increase in the membership of the Church or in rallying a number of men around Mr. White-right and his enterprise. This could be explained, it occurred to me, on the ground that Mr. White-right's time was devoted so largely to his duties as head of the theological college that he was unable to take full advantage of the contacts which the museum and lectures afforded. To all of the work carried on in the court he gave approximately half an hour a day, yet the influence of that work was felt throughout the whole province. In notes made on the visit to Chingchoufu I find my own reaction to my study:

"The results of this work prove conclusively that it is possible to get hold of the literati, and that scientific apparatus and lectures are the means by which we can best attract them. This work is an example of what can be done in a prefectural city, and an indication of what larger things can be accomplished in a provincial capital."

C. H. Robertson was to verify this conclusion. When I met him in Shanghai upon his arrival from America, he informed me that before sailing he had procured a cabinet about the size of an office desk, with which it was possible to perform some one hundred and fifty simple experiments in physics. In view of the unusual demands to be made upon him in his projected work among the literati, I had suggested to him that he take three or, if necessary, four years in Nanking for language study. I thought that

he would have to wait a long time for an opportunity
to use his cabinet.

His language study soon ceased to be carried on
by the usual methods. After only a few weeks he
opened up his cabinet and began to explain in broken
sentences to his language-teacher what was in it and
what he meant to do. The news quickly spread, and
from that time formal language study was impossible. He was likely to be interrupted any time from
seven in the morning until ten at night by visits of
the long-robed literati. They came in numbers of
from one to ten, and a visit sometimes lasted six
hours. Within nine months after his arrival in Nanking he was consulted in the designing and equipping of the science building of the new government
university. Upon its completion a few months later
he gave his first lecture with a demonstration before
His Excellency Liu Kun-yi, the great Viceroy of
the three provinces of which Nanking was the capital.

Three months after his arrival in China he was in
constant contact with members of the literati. Yet he
took seven years of apprenticeship, four in Nanking
and three in Tientsin, the two provincial capitals
having the largest number of resident scholars. At
Tientsin three modern government colleges were having difficulties with their scientific equipment, all of
which he straightened out. Under the patronage of
the enlightened Viceroy Yüan Shih-k'ai, an abandoned Taoist monastery had been transformed into
a modern museum. Its equipment was placed at

Robertson's disposal for use in his lectures anywhere in the city, and he was soon in close touch with the Viceroy and his circle of brilliant returned students from America. As later events proved, contacts at Tientsin and Nanking opened doors to him throughout the whole of the Empire.

In Nanking and Tientsin Robertson discovered the need of apparatus which would enable him to demonstrate before audiences of as many as two thousand persons, and have the farthest observer see the separate parts of the instruments. When he found that no such apparatus could be purchased anywhere to meet this demand, he spent a year and a half in Europe and America building his own apparatus. He laid his problem before many of the leading scientists of the Western world to secure their counsel. Upon his return to China he was ready to begin a nationwide effort.

A few months after the establishment of the Republic he was invited to Wuchang. I accompanied him on this trip. To our surprise Governor-General Li Yüan-hung had arranged to hold the first lecture in his palace and had brought in all of his high officials for the occasion. The General said to Robertson, "Do you remember our first meeting?"

"I'm afraid I do not, Your Excellency," acknowledged Robertson.

"Well, do you remember that lecture you gave reclining on a steamer chair after the coolies had carried you into the auditorium? You had been ill and were not able to stand through the lecture."

"Indeed I do," replied Robertson.

"Do you recall at the end a certain Colonel Li stood up and expressed thanks for the audience?"

"Yes, quite well."

"I was the man," said the General.

So it was that Robertson came to know General Li, who started the revolution which swept the Ch'ing dynasty off the Dragon Throne, became Vice-President, and later President of the Chinese Republic. After he became President, he gave a dinner to Robertson in Peking, and then sent word ahead to the provincial capitals at which Robertson was to lecture, recommending that the largest use be made of his gifts. As a result, there were one hundred thousand people in attendance in ten cities in as many weeks.

The following account of one of Robertson's visits to a smaller provincial capital was given me by Frank Lenz, a colleague of mine in student work:

"Robertson created a sensation when he arrived. He had brought with him seventeen huge trunks containing a radio receiving and sending set, delicate electrical equipment, and a variety of scientific instruments. In fact, his outfit was a cross between a laboratory and a museum; it was a peripatetic classroom designed for popular demonstrations before large or small audiences. He had spent months in America collecting this equipment, and a longer time

in Shanghai designing the cases in which it was to
be transported. He was met at the station by a personal representative of the military governor, who extended an official welcome. Before the antennæ for the
radio had been erected, five editors of local newspapers swooped down upon him for interviews, and
before he could tune in with his mechanician several
school principals had dropped in to 'look see.'

"For five days the lectures continued with morning, afternoon, and evening sessions. Specially invited groups came from the merchant guilds, while
students marched in with bands playing and flags
flying. Several lectures were given for the women,
but the feature of the entire week occurred when
both governors arrived with the leading officials of
the province for a special demonstration of wireless
telephone. Professor Robertson asked Governor Yang
to go across the athletic field to the building where
the sending station was located. He then asked General Chen, the military governor, to mount the platform. The two governors then carried on an ani-
mated conversation. The officials were delighted and
so were the performers. Needless to say our week
ended in a blaze of glory. More than ten thousand
of the educated classes had seen and heard a scientific demonstration that is unique even in the Occident."

The titles to some of Robertson's lectures which
became most famous were: The Gyroscope; Wireless
Telephone and Telegraph; Electrons, Energy, Mat-

ter; The Wonders of Sound; Einstein's Relativity.
One may think that it would be impossible to make
some of these subjects interesting to groups who
were so ignorant of modern science. There was never
an uninteresting moment in these lectures. Through
the courtesy of Mr. Sperry, the inventor, Robertson
had for his demonstration a gyroscope four feet in
height. It was inclosed in a metal case. He would set
it spinning on the rostrum, furnish a wooden staff
and offer a reward to any one in the audience who
would turn it over. There it stood, apparently the
most unstable thing imaginable, and yet members of
the literati who had passed through the ordeal of
nine days of terrific grilling in the examination-halls
and had come out victorious, met their defeat in trying to push over this innocent-looking instrument.

He explained the use of wireless telegraphy. Even
relativity was not only made comprehensible, but intensely interesting. For instance, the lecturer moved
his handkerchief a foot or so across the room and
asked for an opinion as to the actual motion that had
occurred and the consequent velocity. The answer
seemed evident—a distance of one foot in a second of
time. But the lecturer called attention to the fact
that we must take account of the motions due to the
revolution of the earth, its course around the sun,
the movement of the solar system toward some distant point, and the very probable movement of that
distant point to an unknown corner of the universe;

not one foot, but thousands, if not millions of feet in one second of time.

Soon after the visit which Robertson and I made to General Li's headquarters in Wuchang it became necessary to establish in Shanghai a well-equipped laboratory for the manufacture of Robertson's apparatus. As China's adoption of Western civilization increased, the interest of the literati widened and the demand came quite naturally for lectures on a number of aspects of modern culture and medical science. Most of these lectures gained a greater popularity and effectiveness in their presention by the use of apparatus.

It is impossible to estimate justly in quantitative terms the full effect of Robertson's lectures upon the Chinese people. Without question, scientific development has been one of the most significant factors in the impact of Western civilization on China. And it can be no overstatement to say that Robertson's lectures in various branches of science to thousands of the literati—instruction motivated by his lofty ideals and colored by his forceful yet winsome personality —were of great value in enabling his hearers to comprehend the nature of the complex forces coming relentlessly from the West.

The most vivid picture one can now get of the response of the Chinese to Robertson's message is in his own letters and reports, written in brief periods of leisure while on his journeys. The following quotation is from a letter written me during 1929, twenty-seven years after his arrival in China:

"As our northern ship swung into the mouth of the Yangtze and later docked at Shanghai I said, 'Well, that's that!' And what was *that*? It was the end of a ten months' series of lecture journeys covering 12,175 miles in twenty-two great cities of Japan, the Philippines, and China. The attendance totaled 205,600, averaging 643 attendance for 320 lectures.

"In most cities the campaign began slowly. The second day attendance began to mount, and by the last they came in mobs and had to be turned away by thousands. At the first Peking meeting, for instance, the hall was half full; by the third comfortably crowded; and on the last day there were to be meetings at eleven, two, four, and eight o'clock. But then came the National University—they had not received tickets. Could the Association supply them with six hundred?—only by adding another meeting! This was settled for nine in the morning. Back went the president happy with six hundred tickets. Soon he came again, troubled because of six hundred neglected students who insisted on a look-in. Another conference, and another lecture was set for seven in the morning. Then came the head of a school from a distant city on an inspection trip with his students. The only possibility was to admit his group to sit at the back of the room at the technical lecture. Then came the Board of Education head with an urgent request for the three hundred members of his staff.

They were finally squeezed into standing room and divided, a hundred to each of the three afternoon meetings. And that's how it turned out that there were 16,500 attendance—merchants, educators, students, officials—in six days at Peking."

In another letter of the same year Robertson told me of still another lengthy tour:

"From Hangchow. Since we were to have the meeting after eleven in the evening of a stormy day, we were afraid that many would not come. But they came just the same, regardless of the rain and the lateness of the hour. By this you will know how interested the people are.

"Since arriving in Shanghai I have conducted a lecture training conference in which we have swung over such a gamut of subjects as the Gyroscope, the Talking Moving Picture, Citizenship, A Program for the Ideal Life, Spengler's Philosophy of History, Einstein's Relativity, etc. Each student has had opportunity of experiencing: Wave Meter, Electron Measurements, Harmonic Motions, Surface Tension, Air as Lubricant, Radio, and many others. One of the students, returned from American universities, said, 'This is the most interesting course I have ever taken.'

"Soon I begin the administration of a five weeks' course of lecture-training for teachers, 'Y' secretaries, and college graduates in the East China University Union Summer School. It's going to be a big job, and with the latitude of New Orleans it's going

to be hot; but the work will be so stimulatingly interesting that we expect to give the weather a minimum
of attention. . . .

"I'm just home from a Yangtze Valley lecture
tour that took me as far as Changsha, capital of
Hunan, near the center of China. . . . The grim old
city wall was gone and in its place is a belt boulevard, with a wide gash straight across the city's
narrow streets providing another modern communication artery. . . .

"Veryard had scheduled me for a week of lectures
—three a day. Governor Ho Chien and all the high
officials attended the first. His Excellency was so
pleased that he made a request for another week's
stay, but a tight schedule precluded so three extra
lectures were sandwiched in, to be given under the
patronage and as a part of a series of lectures spon-
sored by the Government for its own guests. Our
special Government lectures were the third of a
series, the first being given by the Buddhist leader
of China, and the second by a returned philosopher
from France.

"But even this was not enough to meet the pres-
sure, and so on the last day a popular lecture and a
technical lecture for the Government University had
to be wedged in, which kept things going until midnight. It took a staff of more than two hundred volunteer workers supplemented by a large squad of
police to handle the crowds. That's how it turned
out that not only had we a campaign of quality, but

one of quantity as well—the quantity being represented by an attendance of one in every twenty of
the city's 500,000 population."

As China was emerging from medievalism into the
Modern Age it was not difficult to interest her old
scholars in science; but one may well raise the question—what connection does that have with religion?
In asking for a man with scientific training, my own
thought had been that he would use his science as a
means of gaining confidence and making friends;
then that he would preach to them. That is not what
happened. Robertson spoke as a scientist to men of
education. He did not dilute his science; the same
lectures which he gave to the members of the literati,
he presented later before bodies of distinguished scientists in Europe and America. He did not let
China's backwardness in science lower the high stand-
ards which he had set for the lectures. Nor did he
use science as a means of religious propaganda. But
he was so Christian in his attitude toward the whole
of life that he could not speak without revealing the
underlying religious aspect of his character. When
the question arose as to the application of modern
science to the uses of humanity, Robertson frankly
recognized the peril inherent in the increased physical power placed at man's disposal. Yet in a most
natural manner he held that only by unselfish love
of man for man and by firm confidence in a loving
Heavenly Father could mankind find through science
the boon it seeks.

The story of Robertson's work would fill a volume in itself. The fleeting glimpses I have given are intended merely to show the indispensable part which his work played in my own education, not by giving me a technique for the presentation of science—for I am not a scientist, but by helping me to change fundamentally my conception of my task in China. "Find," Robertson's work seemed to say to me, "that for which men are hungry, and if in itself it is good, give it to them; you can always lead them from a lower to a higher hunger."

Chapter X: The Student Migration

WHEN I left Shanghai in 1904 for a year's furlough in America, China was watching with despair the wave of foreign invasion which was approaching with increased speed and certainty. The huge indemnity exacted after the Boxer war was only the prelude to demands under one pretext or another by nearly all of the great powers. Most Chinese assumed that the war between Russia and Japan, which was then in progress, would result in the defeat of Japan and the division of China among the European powers.

But when I returned toward the end of 1905 I found a new spirit in China. Japan's victory over Russia had been a revelation to China that the European was not superior to the Asiatic in arms. Despair had given way to hope. Even the mass of the illiterate was dimly conscious of some great change. The dragon flag was flying everywhere from buildings and boats. There were parades, celebrations, and patriotic speeches. The national spirit was being born. Changes and reforms in government were the order of the day. Suddenly and without ceremony the old educational system was abolished. A year before, students with a modern education had been discounted; now telegraph wires were humming with messages from officials calling these students to positions of honor and influence. The few modern government colleges established at that time and the missionary colleges were crowded with students. Additional government colleges were opened as rapidly as teachers trained in the new learning could be found. Tsing Hua College, a special institution to prepare students for study in America, was established in Peking, and my friend, Tong Kai-son, who had been a member of the early deputation of Chinese students to America during the Manchu dynasty, was chosen as president. By almost every boat, students were sailing for England, France, Germany, Japan, and America. China had determined to go to school to the world.

On the new road which China was taking, Japan was the acknowledged guide. Teachers from Japan were being brought in by the hundreds to supply the faculties of the new government institutions. But the most remarkable indication of Japan's influence was the exodus of Chinese students to Tokyo. They went from every section of the Chinese Empire, including Manchuria and Mongolia, many even making the long journey from the borders of Annam, Burma, and Tibet. They were of all ages from fifteen to sixty. A large number of the older men had already gained distinction in classical scholarship, but they felt the need for the new learning and were eager to study every phase of it.

As I passed through Tokyo on the return to China, I found Japan perplexed as how to take care of this flood of Chinese students. For the most part they had never been abroad, and many of them had not traveled even in their own country; few of them could speak a foreign language. Thus the people in Japan who wished to be of some service to the Chinese students were prevented by the obstacle of language. What added to Japan's difficulty was the fact that the cessation of the war with Russia had released the Japanese soldiers in Manchuria, who were pouring back by the thousands, filling all barracks, hotels, and every available lodging-place. The Chinese students consequently experienced great difficulty in finding suitable living-quarters and often became victims of the worst element in the community. I was urged by the Japanese Christians and the missionaries there to advise the Christian leaders in Shanghai to take immediate practical measures for relieving this alarming situation.

Upon my arrival in Shanghai I laid the problem before my colleague, D. Willard Lyon, who agreed to go to Tokyo and study the situation. His lucid and forceful statement, made after a month of investigation, revealed an opportunity of urgency and importance. As a result of his report, twenty leading missionaries of China prepared an appeal to the missionary societies of all Christian lands to coöperate in service for this group of students in Tokyo. Several societies whose representatives were authorized to speak for their boards gave immediate favorable response. Bishop J. W. Bashford, a far-seeing statesman, offered to furnish the missionary of his Church best qualified to assist in the undertaking. Bishop Logan H. Roots of the American Episcopal Mission in Hankow gave an equally strong indorsement and released the pastor of a large church to proceed at once to Tokyo. The authorities of other British and American missionary societies gave full coöperation as the program developed. The responsibility for assembling the staff to administer this undertaking fell to me.

It was agreed that the Chinese worker to head the whole enterprise needed three qualifications: first, a thorough knowledge of the Christian religion and a passion for furthering it; second, a mastery of Chinese classical learning which would command the respect of the literati; and third, a modern education to enable him to assist the students in their adjustment to a modern world. In my first survey of the situation I had almost come to the conclusion that there was no such man in China. Few members of the literati had become Christians, and of these almost none were equipped with the new learning. But Mr. C. T. Wang, principal of a modern government school in Changsha, the capital city of Hunan province located five hundred miles up the Yangtze, had been highly recommended by several people in whose judgment I had confidence. He was the son of a Church of England pastor, had a thorough training in the Chinese classics, and was a graduate of the provincial college at Tientsin, a modern institution. Upon Wang's arrival in Shanghai on a visit to his family I arranged an interview with him, but with little hope of a favorable outcome. He came into my office, a young man under twenty-five, alert, athletic, and decisive. We had been together but a short time before I felt that I could dispense with the usual Oriental preliminaries, lay the Tokyo mission before him and ask him to undertake the task. I did so briefly. He saw its possibilities at once.

"There could be no greater opportunity for service," he said, "but I don't know what I ought to do. The Governor of Hunan has just offered me a scholarship which will pay all of my expenses at Yale University for four years. My course at Tientsin, fortunately, gave me English, which enables me to take advantage of the Governor's proposal. This is my one opportunity to secure a foreign education. As you know, I am the son of a minister and I have a wife and two children. I have no money. If my country is to meet the demands of its new day, it must have men with a thorough foreign education as well as Chinese training. Have I the right to decline the Governor's offer?"

For a few moments I thought over what he had said. He was right in assuming that his country must have men who had been educated abroad. I did not have a dollar to match the Governor's gift; but I believed that the opportunity in Tokyo was boundless. The decision had to be made immediately, and I resolved to share the risk with Mr. Wang.

"I do not know that you are willing, upon such a brief acquaintance, to trust my word in a matter which means so much to your future, but I wish to make this proposal. You go to Tokyo for two years. That will be the important period. You can map out the plans and find other leaders. At the end of that time, I promise to give you an opportunity to have four years in an American college. I cannot promise Yale, but the college will be a first-class institution. You must understand that I too am a poor man. I have no authority to pledge any one and can give you no guarantee but my word. This may mean that I retire from my missionary work and go into business. If so, I will earn while you study. You must see how strongly I feel about your going to Tokyo."

"I will give you my answer tomorrow after I have conferred with Mrs. Wang."

He came back the next day and said, "I will go."

When I joined him in Japan a few months later, we went together to interview the leading officials and educators of the country, including Marquis Saionji, the Premier, and Mr. Makino, Minister of Education. All were unanimous in expressing their appreciation of our proposed Christian work in behalf of the Chinese students. I recall particularly our interview with Count Okuma, founder of Waseda University. He came in limping as the result of a gunshot wound inflicted by a would-be assassin while he was Premier. In his remarks he was outspoken but cordial.

"In caring for this great host of Chinese students we must have the help of every Christian country. When we sent our students to America," he said to me, "you took them into your Christian homes. You let them see Christian civilization at its best. What can we do for these Chinese students? We have no Christian homes into which to take them. In any case our customs would not admit of our taking strange young men into the home. The situation is in desperate need of the help of Christians all over the world."

Then he turned to Wang and, for more than a quarter of an hour, voiced with impassioned eloquence his personal debt to China. He described his education as a long period of drinking at the fount of Confucian culture.

"Everything we have in Japan," he concluded, "we owe to you. How can we ever pay back our debt? I am glad that there is some small service which we can render to your students at the present time. But how shallow is our civilization in comparison to yours!"

During this manifestly sincere tribute to China I glanced at Wang's face and found him in tears. Count Okuma and Wang had met on a common basis of Confucian culture. Proud of this common heritage, they were intensely moved and found between themselves at once a deep harmony. Yet understanding that fact, neither one suggested that in Confucian doctrine he could find a way out of this present situation. In this hour of crisis both were turning to Christianity.

Though I scarcely realized all the implications of this tacit acceptance at the time, this same phenomenon was recurring all over China where thinking people were seeking moral guidance in a troubled time. Nor was it until many years afterwards, during which I had reflected with growing intensity upon the highly moral nature of the Confucian teachings, that I appreciated and understood the full significance of that affecting meeting between Count Okuma and Wang.

After the interview Wang said to me as we walked out of the gate, "I have never been more deeply moved."

He was afterward to become Minister of Foreign Affairs, and for many years was a powerful influence in determining the foreign policy of China. While no official of the government could have withstood the aggression of the foreign powers more heroically, Wang always insisted that friendship between China and Japan should be a fixed policy on the part of both countries.

In dealing with the unexpected influx of Chinese students, whose number in Tokyo soon reached fifteen thousand, the government officials and educational authorities of Japan gave to Wang during the following months abundant evidence of their tact, resourcefulness and coöperation. In addition to the liberal assistance to Wang and his associates, the Japanese government met the sudden flood of foreign students with a solicitude, forethought, and expedition rare in my observation. Some idea of the magnitude of the task of providing for the welfare of these students may be gained from the fact that, within a few months' time, the government accomplished the building and equipping of several whole colleges, where only flat land had been before. These colleges were exclusively for the visiting Chinese students and were provided with complete faculties of Japanese professors. The spirit permeating this whole movement impressed me with the kindliness of the Japanese.

The Japanese Church also recognized its responsibility to these Chinese students. One pastor devoted himself entirely to the students, learning the Chinese language and making his headquarters in the building of the Chinese Christian Student Movement. The Japanese Y. M. C. A. placed its commodious auditorium at Wang's disposal on Sunday evenings. Several of the Japanese pastors attracted to their churches Chinese students who had mastered the Japanese language sufficiently to follow the sermons.

With characteristic thoroughness and dispatch Wang soon inaugurated practical measures for improving the situation among the Chinese students.

An Information Bureau was organized in Shanghai where students could get advice as to necessary preparations for the journey, and learn how to get in touch with the Student Movement representatives who would meet the boat at Yokohama. Arrangements were made, accordingly, to have the boats met as they docked at Yokohama, the students accompanied to the Student Movement headquarters in Tokyo and directed thence to approved lodgings. Because of the close contacts established with Japanese educational authorities, Wang and his colleagues were able to advise the students as to choice of colleges and courses of study. The program of work covered a wide range of religious teaching and social service. It included the introduction of the students into the unknown world of athletics and physical training in the gymnasium, the conduct of classes in English in response to a demand beyond the power of the Japanese educational authorities to supply, the provision of popular lectures, the distribution of Christian literature, the holding of regular church services by the two Chinese pastors, Bible classes, weekly meetings in the auditorium, and extended student conferences during the summer vacation.

The field of work was not confined strictly to students. Frequently deputations of educators from different parts of China went to Japan to study the educational system. The attention which the Movement showed to forty-eight educators of Chihli will

illustrate how the opportunity of such visits was util-
ized. While the party, made up of twenty-nine
county commissioners of education, seven principals
of schools, and twelve officials and teachers, were in
Tokyo, the Student Movement lent them a hall in
which to hold the lectures delivered to them by Japanese educators. It also held two receptions in their
honor, arranged for lectures on religion, and in other
ways came into close touch with them. The educators
heartily appreciated the efforts made in their behalf,
and not a few confessed that their conception of
Christianity had been changed during their stay.
The leader of the party, after his return to China,
became a baptized Christian.

On a later visit to Tokyo I attended one of the
Sunday evening meetings. The auditorium was filled
with the students similarly dressed in grey uniforms,
and of all ages, from youths in their teens to men of
sixty. Wang spoke to them for more than an hour on
the subject, What China Needs. As he approached
the end he compared America and China. His picture
of conditions in America was idealized and much
more favorable than was justified, but he was sincere.
He contrasted its freedom, plenty, optimism, democracy and spirit of self-sacrifice, with the situation in
China. He portrayed the corruption of officials in
China, where money must open the gate to prefer-
ment. He described the conservatism, bigotry and ignorance of modern learning on the part of the liter-

ati, the poverty and widespread illiteracy among the people. He explained China's sorry place among the nations of the world.

At times he was pitiless in denunciation; at times his voice softened and his words were filled with pathos. He drew illustrations from both the Bible and the Chinese classics. To drive home his points he quoted Confucius, Abraham Lincoln, and Jesus. He denounced the corruption, ignorance, bigotry, and selfishness in China, but not the religions. He declared Christianity as the hope of the country in the crisis through which it was passing. He described George Washington, his courage, ability, and humility. He told briefly the story of how Washington had won his country's freedom against overwhelming odds.

"Why," he asked, "did George Washington make such a sacrifice? I will tell you why. Because he was a Christian. He had before him the picture of Jesus Christ who died on a cross that he might save mankind. That is what China must have. Christianity will give us officials who, like George Washington, are willing to be the servants of the people."

During the next two years this auditorium was to be Wang's pulpit, and from it most of the Chinese students in Tokyo heard his message.

After Wang had been in Japan about a year and a half, I made a visit to Tokyo and raised with him the question as to his staying a third year. He felt it essential to hold to his program and proceed with his graduate work abroad. Up to that time I had not been able to make provision for his scholarship. But as I was returning by rail from Tokyo to Nagasaki en route to Shanghai, I noticed a party of four American tourists, evidently two men and their wives. With the burden of securing Wang's scholarship on my mind, I decided to make their acquaintance and, in spite of the embarrassment of making a financial appeal to utter strangers, to tell them about Wang and my promise to him.

I learned that they were from Lansing, Michigan, that they were on their way to Manila, and that upon their return they expected to remain for several weeks in Japan. The two men were members of the Board of Directors of the Lansing Young Men's Christian Association, which had just erected a new building free of debt, and this trip was in celebration of the event. I told them my mission and asked them to meet Wang upon their return to Tokyo.

Some six weeks later I had a letter from one of them saying, "We have met Mr. Wang, and we will consider it a privilege to provide the scholarship fund which you suggested, so that he may have his four years of study in America."

In the giving of my early promise to Wang and in his acceptance of it, we both risked much. But the promise had been made good, and my associations with him in his work in Tokyo are now among the

richest memories I cherish; not the least of these is
that of the visit to Count Okuma.

On a visit to Tokyo in the winter of 1910 I conducted a series of evangelistic meetings among the
Chinese students there. I will quote briefly from notes
written shortly after that visit:

"I think I may say that in my nearly twenty years
of work among students I have never seen such remarkable interest in religion as was manifested during my five days in Tokyo. The first meeting was in
the new Waseda Dormitory. They had three rooms
thrown together and these were crowded; men were
standing in the vestibule, and even lined up on the
stairs outside. I spoke for about an hour and a quarter on 'How I Came to a Belief in Jesus Christ.'
When I asked those to rise who were willing, in spite
of opposition of family, friends, government, and
the demands of self, to do the will of God, more
than half of the audience stood up. I had put the
question with as much care as I could, and the men
seemed to understand fully what they were doing.
After this the meeting was dismissed. As I remember
it, not a single man left. The meeting was then
thrown open for questions, and with Oriental passion and vehemence they poured question after question into me. After this had continued for considerable time, the meeting was again dismissed. It was
dismissed even a third time, and after about three

hours I withdrew, leaving a crowd of earnest inquirers around Wallace (the secretary in charge)."

Throughout my experience in China and, more recently, in Japan, I had marveled at the eagerness of the students to discuss religion as it applied to them personally. These further lines from my Tokyo notes reveal the intensity of this eagerness:

"At the last meeting there were fifteen hundred students present. I spoke for an hour and a half, and if I had asked for an expression, I verily believe that one thousand men would have responded; but our force of men for following up the meeting was so small that I felt it was wise not to call for any such expression.

"The present conditions in China have brought the students almost to a state of hopelessness, and when one is able to show them that there is in Christianity a way out of the present difficulties, their readiness to accept it is phenomenal. Before leaving, a meeting of two hours was held with the Christians and the recent converts.

"One of the most difficult things I have ever had to do was to decline to see men who were literally pleading with me for further conference about their souls' welfare. Some of the inquirers followed me clear to the depot."

It would be difficult to overestimate the influence of the returned students upon China during the decade between 1910 and 1920. They became presidents and faculty members of the colleges which sprung up in the capital cities like mushrooms after a rain. They were in the large majority among teachers of secondary education. They edited the newspapers and wrote the modern books. They were the predominant force in the provisional government organized under Sun Yat-sen following the Revolution.

In 1912 I made a visit to Nanking, the capital of the government. C. T. Wang was there as a member of the Senate. He had graduated from Yale the year before and had returned to China to become head of the Student Christian Movement. Discussing with Wang the important part the returned students were taking in the new China, I asked, "How many members of the Senate are returned students?"

"Nine-tenths," he replied, "most of them from Japan."

I found them quite as much in evidence on the Board of Education and the Board of Finance; in fact, they were represented on all the government boards. They later became an equally effective force in the Republic.

In my travel over China from year to year I not only studied the general influence which they exerted upon the nation, but followed many of them individually. I was impressed that as a rule the returned students who exercised the deepest influence and gave the greatest promise of usefulness to their country had two general characteristics in common: they were

Christians, and they had had a thorough grounding in the Confucian discipline. Onto their Christian faith they had grafted their early Confucian learning, which found there a nutritive element that revealed the present-day value of their own culture.

Chapter XI: Mapping the Course of a New Civilization

By 1908 the modernization of China had become the accepted goal of the nation. The Westerners who had declared that China would never change were amazed at the pace with which she went forward and the wide front of the transformation. Education, industry, government, social institutions—everything must become modern, and that at once.

The spirit of reform, so evident on the part of the people, failed to influence the Manchu government, which continued inefficient and corrupt. In fact, following the death of the Empress Dowager, it had rapidly deteriorated. The Prince Regent, ignorant, weak, and proud, was under the domination of a palace clique. Bribery had never been so open nor so potent. Moreover, the Manchu oligarchy, conscious of its weakness and of the growing dissatisfaction of the Chinese people, made the tactical blunder of widening the gulf between the Manchu and the Chinese; the government positions of greater influence were gradually taken from Chinese and given to Manchus. It soon became clear that the promised constitutional government was being delayed as long as possible. Students of affairs in China saw that a conflict was inevitable.

Serious outbreaks developed in three capital cities, Canton, Changsha, and Chengtu. While two of the revolts collapsed, the one at Chengtu did not abate. The torrent of reform was dashing headlong against the stone wall of Manchu conservatism and corruption. Would the torrent be stayed, or would the wall give way?

The collapse of the Manchu Dynasty in 1911 brought only a partial answer, for freedom from Manchu control did not mean freedom at once from the consequences of that control. Until almost the end the government had discouraged efforts to train leaders for the new era. The Chinese Educational Commission, founded in 1872 by Doctor Yung Wing for the purpose of sending annually a group of Chinese students to America for a period of six to eight years of study, had been abolished within a few years after its establishment, and the students trained under it had been disregarded or disgraced. The reformers of 1898, who wished to modernize the educational requirements for official positions, had been beheaded or sent in exile. The ship of state, now fortunately rid of its ignorant captain, was sailing a rough and unknown sea, short of mariners and without chart or compass.

The small Christian community furnished a majority of those who were prepared to take the helm and develop new leaders. The nation was eager to accept their guidance. The Christian colleges in China had provided a modern education and for a period of years had sent some of their most promising graduates to Europe or America for further study. The fact that the Revolution was so largely bloodless was in part due to the influence of Christians. They also brought an early end to the vengeful barbarities practiced against the Manchus. Even leaders who were not Christians attributed to God the speedy success of the Revolution. All over China, from the mouths of Christians and non-Christians, in the press and in the Provisional Parliament, Christianity was being proclaimed the basis for a permanent Republic.

The Christians were quick to appreciate both the peril and the opportunity of the new situation. For several months the question engaged the attention of a group of the most thoughtful Christian leaders among the returned students in Shanghai. They called me into consultation and presented the situation somewhat as follows:

The Christians who have had a thorough modern education are too few in number to supply but a small proportion of the demand for men in government, education, finance, business, and industry. What we might do, and do at once, in helping China adjust herself to the present situation is to interpret to the leaders of the nation the deeper meaning of modern civilization, to define the nature of the changes which must be made, to outline the new educational policy, to evaluate China's cultural heritage in the light of the new learning, and to reveal the spirit in which the renaissance should be carried forward. This needs to be done on a nation-wide scale and to be carried forward with rapidity. It must be done by men able to speak with authority and it must be a mission to leaders, not to the mass of the people.

The group suggested the organization of a National Lecture Bureau composed of Christian leaders from different parts of the country. They expressed the belief that Robertson's work furnished a technique which could be applied on a wider front. The first and perhaps the most difficult problem was to discover, as the head of the bureau, a distinguished man whose leadership would be nationally recognized. They commissioned me to secure this man. I discussed the problem with Bishop Roots of Hankow.

"I know the man to head the Bureau," he said. "David Yui."

"He would be splendid, but how can we get him from the government?" I inquired. "General Li would not release him."

"Yui would take it. He has every prospect of advancement in the government, but his heart is in distinctly Christian work."

I remembered David Z. T. Yui very well as a quiet, thoughtful delegate to a student conference held some years before at Kuling. In the meantime he had graduated from Wuchang College, St. John's University in Shanghai, and Harvard University, where he had taken his Master's Degree *cum laude* in education, and had won a prize of five hundred dollars

for excellence in scholarship. I knew his father, a
Chinese scholar and a preacher in the Episcopal
Church, who had insisted that his son must master
the classics as well as secure a modern education.
Upon his return to China Yui had been made head
of the Department of Foreign Affairs in the provisional government established by Governor-General
Li Yüan-hung. With the smallest possible delay I arranged an interview with him.

When the situation was laid before Yui, he gave a
favorable response. Before long he had mapped out
comprehensive plans for the effective expansion of
the Lecture Bureau. Robertson was to continue his
scientific lectures. Dr. John Y. Lee, a graduate of
the University of Chicago, where he had been associated with Doctor Michelson in research in optics
and with Doctor Millikan in the isolation of the electron, joined Doctor Yui as head of the laboratory
and gave special attention to designing and develop-
ing scientific apparatus. Doctor Yui himself was to
lecture on the modernization of Chinese education.
Dr. D. Y. Lin, a returned student from America who
had specialized in Forestry at Yale University, was
called to head the Department of Conservation of
Natural Resources. Dr. M. Thomas Tchou, the son
of an official in Szechwan and a graduate of the University of Edinburgh, joined the staff to deal with
the problems of the new economic adjustment. He
was an accomplished linguist, speaking Chinese,
English, French, and German, with equal fluency. Dr.

Herman C. E. Liu, now the able president of the
University of Shanghai, was placed in charge of the
Department of Citizenship Training, and Dr. W. W.
Peter, because of his conspicuous service in the
American Red Cross and his genius for organization,
was asked to head the Department of Health Edu-
cation.

Although in his direction of this educational effort
Doctor Yui rendered a notable service to China, his
most conspicuous contribution was in his own lectures. I remember some of my trips with him as
among my most rewarding experiences. Often the
program arranged covered from twelve to sixteen
hours a day. Receptions by the boards of trade, educational associations, Young Men's Christian Associations, chambers of commerce, and the missionary
communities would come in rapid succession, and Yui
would speak at each gathering.

One of the first acts of the new government had
been to establish modern colleges in Peking and in
all the provincial capitals, and the leaders of the
nation were in great need of an authoritative voice
on modern education. Consequently, Doctor Yui's
lectures on education were welcomed by officials and
educators alike. On his visits to the capital cities he
was given full opportunity to meet with the officials
of the government and the faculties of the colleges.
Upon his arrival the Governor would assemble all
provincial officials and staffs, sometimes numbering
two or three hundred, and Yui would speak for sev-

eral hours to them. This would be followed by similar meetings with the educational authorities.

Doctor Yui's message was equally acceptable to the older members of the literati and the modern students. While his approach was philosophic, his speeches were always well-balanced and logical, and he was an eloquent speaker. He related modern education to China's rich heritage of the past. He could describe the splendor of China's past and point out the possibilities for the future in contrast with the plight of the present in such a way that his audiences were sometimes moved to tears, but he always closed on a hopeful note. Other speakers presented their themes ofttimes without making direct religious application, but Yui never had any misgivings about driving home the religious application; nor was this ever resented by his large and influential Confucian audiences. Their primary concern was the rebirth of their native land, the regeneration of national life, and their interest in Christianity began from the consideration of it as a means to that end.

D. Y. Lin's lectures on forestry readily lent themselves to the use of Robertson's technique in his demonstrated science lectures. After Lin's apparatus had been prepared in the Shanghai laboratory, I attended one of his first presentations. On the platform beside the speaker the attendants placed the model of a village situated at the foot of a high hill down which in a gorge flowed a little stream. Beneath the village were fields of rice and beans, and a grove of

mulberry trees to furnish food for the silkworms.
The ancestral hall, the temple, the tile-covered roofs
of the rich and the thatch-covered roofs of the poor,
made a charming picture. Lin gave a brief description of the delights of village life. Then he called
attention to the denuded hill that towered above the
village: the ancient trees that had stood there for
several hundred years had been cut down almost
to the last one. Suddenly the audience was startled
by a flash of lightning, a burst of thunder, and a
downpour of rain. This torrent filled the gorge,
washed away the village, and flooded the fields with
water and debris.

For an hour and a half Lin drove home, in part by
such vivid objective presentation and in part by convincing words, the mistake which had been made in
denuding the hills of China, and emphasized the urgent need for reforestation. He connected the disas-
ters with which the Chinese were so familiar in the
Yellow River and the Yangtze River valleys with the
destruction of the forests. Thus from the subject of
forestry and its relation to floods, famine, and disease, he carried the audience to a consideration of
conservation of all natural resources in China. Lin
soon found himself overwhelmed with invitations from
governors of provinces, mayors of cities, magistrates,
and other officials who wished to have him educate
their officials as well as the people.

A natural resource to which Lin could give only
passing mention, namely national health, commanded

the entire attention of another department of the Lecture Bureau. At that time China had no vital statistics, no quarantine laws except in ports under the maritime customs, no boards of health, no health laws, and no coöperative effort to avoid such diseases as tuberculosis, cholera, plague, typhus, and hookworm. The Chinese people had come to realize that these diseases were not caused by the power of an inexorable fate, and they felt the need of health education. There was probably no subject, not even politics, which was so popular in China in the early days of the Republic as the elimination of preventable diseases. The Lecture Bureau received more requests for lectures along this line than any other.

The purpose of the health education department of the Lecture Bureau was to take advantage of this awakened interest in the prevention of disease, and to educate, organize, and direct it into practical methods for the conservation of human resources of the nation. The department would present through lectures a task to be performed by the community.

Very soon after Doctor Peter had joined Doctor Yui's staff an epidemic of cholera broke out in Foochow which taxed all of his powers of initiative and imagination. The previous year this dread disease had caused fifty thousand deaths in the city. The present epidemic had appeared earlier in the year and reports indicated that it threatened to be much more serious. Fears were expressed that it might almost decimate the population of the city. No time

could be lost, so Doctor Peter caught the first boat
to Foochow, and took with him a staff of assistants
from the laboratory. The Governor, who had spent
ten thousand dollars the year before in an idol procession to expel the cholera spirit, offered Doctor
Peter every coöperation.

Doctor Peter studied the situation. The cholera
germ was spread by flies; the whole secret lay there.
The flies infested the great market-place; they
swarmed over the fresh fruit displayed on the coun-
ters of thousands of tiny shops. If he could eliminate
the flies, he could stop the cholera. But the city had a
population of one million people, of whom there were
probably not five hundred who knew the relation between the flies and the cholera germ. Doctor Peter
said to himself: "My task is huge but simple. Within
ten days I must teach one million people two sentences: Filth causes flies. Flies cause cholera."

He began by enlisting the help of the officials, the
universities, the Chamber of Commerce and the
churches. He had a committee of coöperation numbering two thousand five hundred, headed by the
Governor. Posters were pasted on every available
space. Every theater in the city, the auditoriums of
the universities, colleges, and schools, were requisitioned for lectures, and students and professors in
government and mission educational institutions were
trained to make brief addresses to the people. The
attendance at these lectures rose steadily from ten
thousand up to fifty thousand a day. A mammoth

parade was arranged in which fifty thousand people took part. At the head of the procession were floats bearing enormous models of flies, some five feet in length and correspondingly high. They looked as terrifying as tigers. Another series of floats illustrated the effect of the cholera germ at work. On the first float were pieces of watermelon with flies on them. On the second was a man eating the watermelon. On the third float a man was writhing in the agonies of cholera. The fourth float bore his coffin.

In one week at least three hundred and fifty thousand people were taught the cause of cholera and how to prevent it. The result was that the epidemic was stopped, and there were after that only a few sporadic cases. After the close of the campaign the shopkeepers put in glass fronts or netting to protect the food from flies. The rubbish piles were cleaned up. Months afterward when in Foochow I noticed signs reading "Sanitary Watermelons," "Sanitary Restaurants." The word "sanitary," unknown before, had become one of the most popular words in the city.

The Lecture Bureau took on an aspect which Doctor Yui had not contemplated. He had primarily developed the organization with the interests of the literati in mind. But with such undeniable demands upon its resources as that made by the cholera epidemic, mass education for illiterate adults seemed a short and logical step. Although the relationship was there before us, its full significance was not really comprehended until the idea of mass education was advanced by Y. C. James Yen (Jimmie Yen), in whose heart it had been born.

I first met Yen in 1903 while conducting evangelistic meetings at the University of Hongkong. After the opening meeting a student came to my room. He had become a Christian, he told me, through the influence of an English missionary in Szechwan and had come to Hongkong to prepare himself for a university course in America. He wanted me to advise him about his college and his future work. It was Yen, a slender youth with intellectual face and a striking winsomeness of manner. My heart was strangely drawn to him.

We kept in close touch with each other after he went to Yale. During the World War he interrupted his course to go to France, where he and a few other students volunteered to work among the contingent of Chinese coolies whom the Allies had taken there to serve as laborers in the building of trenches. Yen and one of his colleagues attempted to teach these illiterate coolies a thousand Chinese characters. As part of that interesting experiment they edited a newspaper which used only these thousand basic characters.

When the World War was over and the Chinese labor battalion had gone back to China, Yen returned to America, completed his course at Yale, and took a year of post-graduate work at Princeton. One

day I said to him: "Now you are ready to go back
to work among the students of China. Your training
in the Chinese classics under your father, your family name, and your education abroad will give you
a place of national leadership at once. You have a
mission to China's scholars."

Most considerately but with finality he replied:
"No, my future is settled. It was settled when I was
in France working with the coolies. I decided definitely to give my life, not to the literati, but to the
poorest and most ignorant."

He had thought through the whole question, not
only as to his goal, but the practical measures which
were necessary to accomplish it.

"Is China to be a democracy?" he continued. "She
cannot be a democracy simply by overthrowing the
Manchus. Ninety per cent of the people of China
cannot read or write their own language. Can it succeed as a democracy? China's illiterate millions must
be educated right away. A great step has been
taken," he explained, "by the literary revolution
which has abolished the classical language and
adopted the spoken language as the present literary
medium. This facilitates and simplifies the study of
the Chinese language. But a practical plan to eliminate illiteracy has not been devised. The uplift of the
nation means the uplift of the masses. Consequently,
free schools for illiterate children and adults have
sprung up like mushrooms all over the country, but
few concrete results have been achieved. The prob-

lem has not been thought through. If we are to deal with our illiterate millions, two essentials are required; first, an educational tool, and second, an educational campaign."

"What do you mean by an educational tool?" I asked.

"We must have something which will make reading much easier. From my experience in France I have come to the conclusion that one thousand characters, if scientifically selected, would form a working vocabulary which would enable a man to write business letters, keep accounts, and read simple newspapers intelligently. In France my colleague, Daniel C. Fu, and I selected a thousand characters, taught them to the laborers, and then issued a *Laborers' Weekly*. Our selection was not scientific, but even so the *Laborers' Weekly* proved enormously popular, and Fu and I found that through this medium we could express most of the things we wished to say to the laborers. If the characters were scientifically chosen and a literature prepared for the common people, the problem of making China literate would be comparable to that of making a European country literate. As it is now, gaining the ability to read intelligently in China is about equal in difficulty to attaining a high-school education in America or Europe.

"Having worked out the tool, we shall need to discover some device to put it into effective operation. To promote an educational program for over three hundred and sixty million illiterates, one must have organized coöperative effort. The work must be done largely by the help of volunteer workers; we can get these if we interest them. If educated persons will give two hours a day for a period of four months to teaching illiterates, China can be made literate in an incredibly short time. Moreover, if the literates will render this service of educating the poor and ignorant, they will at the same time develop themselves by sharing their possessions with their less privileged brothers and sisters."

My first reaction was to try to dissuade Yen from an impossible undertaking. But I soon saw that his life was irrevocably committed to it and that he had thought through the problem with a thoroughness that was amazing. "You will need to perfect your tool," I told him, "and there are scholars in China who will coöperate with you in that. As to the second essential in your plan, had you not better join David Yui? Is there not much in the technique of that work to help you in your educational campaign?" He agreed with me and returned to China to confer with David Yui.

About a year afterwards I was visiting Changsha, Hunan Province. When I first went out to China, Hunan had been the only province in the Yangtze Valley which no foreigner could enter; it had been a hotbed of opposition to Christianity. By this time its attitude had greatly changed and it had become the center of Yale-in-China, but the Christian community was young and not yet well established. One of the foreign missionaries asked me, "Do you know that man Jimmie Yen of Shanghai?"

"Yes," I replied.

"Well, he is making the most amazing and impossible demands upon all of us. He came here some time ago and said that he wanted Changsha to be the first city to demonstrate what could be done to teach illiterates to read within a few months' time. He persuaded us to promise our coöperation. Our goal is to teach one thousand illiterates in one hundred classes to read and write one thousand characters. The whole course is to be completed in four months with daily sessions of only one to one and a half hours. During his brief preliminary visit to the city he organized a general committee of seventy-five men, including college presidents, editors, officers, guild leaders, merchants, and pastors. We all went in for it. But his letters and telegrams imply that he expects everybody to stop all other work."

"Take my advice," I said to him. "Do everything Yen suggests. You are not only working for Changsha, but you are setting an example to the whole country."

Everywhere in the city I saw large posters picturing China's problem of illiteracy and the need of education. A little later the Governor issued a proclamation urging all citizens who had illiterate children or apprentices to see that they availed themselves of the opportunity to learn. Twenty-six thousand handbills were distributed urging the people to secure an education and giving information about the Foundation Character Schools. The newspapers gave much display space to the campaign.

After Yen returned to the city, a mass meeting was called at which the Governor presided. College and middle-school students paraded through the city carrying large banners and lanterns with inscriptions such as these: *Is your son blind? Can you endure to see three-fourths of China go blind? An illiterate nation is a weak nation.*

All of this was good for creating sentiment, but Yen never left anything to chance. There might be a great deal of enthusiasm among the educated classes, but the uneducated people had to be aroused. They were to be the pupils. In the plan for recruiting them the city was divided into seventy-five districts. Teams of college and middle-school students were trained and sent with registration cards to visit shops and homes. From among the faculties of the educational institutions eighty teachers were recruited. Every teacher was required to be a normal-school or high-school graduate, with three or more years' teaching experience. Each evening one hour would be devoted to a study of the thousand characters, and the rest of the time divided between singing and talks on moral problems. No teacher would receive any salary, but would be given an allowance for his jinricksha fare.

Another important item was to secure meeting-places. The committee in charge requisitioned primary schools, churches, guild-halls, temples, club-houses, private residences, the Y. M. C. A., and other places. The school term lasted from March through June. Twelve hundred boys and men attended regularly and took the final examinations. Nine hundred and sixty-seven passed, and were given certificates by the Governor of the province in the presence of an enormous audience brought together for the graduating exercises.

I have described this first campaign with some detail. It gives a good idea of the combination of popular appeal and thoroughness which characterized all of Yen's work. It is interesting to note that two months later Changsha followed up the great effort of the spring with another campaign, enrolling fourteen hundred students. When the final examination was held, four months later, a thousand and ten passed successfully and the town once more celebrated with a huge Commencement.

What took place in Changsha was soon duplicated in city after city over the whole country. I remember a meeting held in the largest theater in Hankow where Yen spoke before the educated members of the community, appealing to them to sacrifice in behalf of the poor and the illiterate. He called for volunteers to give two hours a day for four months in teaching the illiterates. About two thousand five hundred educated people in Hankow volunteered for service in the campaign.

Some years later Marshal Chang of Manchuria in-

vited Yen to inaugurate mass education in the Man-
churian army. After our stay in Mukden on this
errand we went to Harbin, the northernmost city of
Manchuria, a city that reminded one of Dallas and
Kansas City in the 'nineties. Its population was composed of people from Siberia, Mongolia, Russia,
Japan, and China. The Russian settlement alone
numbered one hundred thousand. The city was filled
with the pioneer spirit; the people dared to do big
things. Yen's reputation had preceded him. We were
met at the train by a body of distinguished citizens
and the city's brass band, its members dressed in
brilliant Oriental color. Dr. C. C. Wang, president
of the Chinese Eastern Railway and the first citizen
of the city, took Yen and me from the station to his
palatial residence, where we were his guests during
our stay. Meetings had been arranged for Yen at
restaurants and hotels, where large and important
audiences gathered both at luncheon and dinner.
His speeches were masterly. The Chinese classics
were on the tip of his tongue; the Bible was equally
at his command.

So revolutionary in the thought life of the nation
was the program of the National Lecture Bureau
that one could not do justice to its story in a little
space. My purpose in the account I have given is to
illustrate the relation which existed at this time between Christian and Confucian leaders in China. Dr.
David Yui and his colleagues were fired with consciousness of the profound crisis through which the

nation was passing, and believed passionately that
Christianity was the only force which would enable
China to make the necessary adjustment to the new
era. Their audiences, predominantly Confucian,
seemed to think it perfectly natural that these
patriots should speak with such earnestness, and it
was from these audiences that new leaders came to
devote themselves to the task of creating a new
China.

The Lecture Bureau was organized as a distinctly
Christian enterprise. The laymen who composed the
Board and all the lecturers were Christian. This
policy was not inaugurated with any sense of superiority on the part of the Christians or any lack of
a spirit of sharing with those of other faiths. It
was considered essential in order to enable Christians
to make their distinctive contribution to the need of
the hour. That the policy met with the approval of
the Confucianists was shown by their whole-hearted
coöperation; the fact that it was Christian aroused
no prejudice against it among the Confucianists. The
Christians saw more clearly than any other group
in the nation the fundamental changes which were
necessary in China's readjustment, and the spirit
and methods by which the changes were to be effected.
The Lecture Bureau was a rapid means of education
rather than an instrument for the conduct of the
enterprises to which it directed attention. It wisely
confined its efforts primarily to education. For the

application of the principles which it enunciated to
the program of reconstruction, it generously gave
its personnel to the government and to voluntary
organizations composed both of Christians and those
of other faiths. Doctor Lin was released to the government to become head of the Department of Forestry, organized through his influence by the province of Shantung. Doctor Peter was asked to be
Secretary of the National Health Association, which
he helped to organize, and later, Adviser on Public
Health to the national government. Doctor Tchou
joined the government as Adviser to the Department of Industry, and Doctor Yen became head of
the Chinese National Association of the Mass Education Movement. Of this Movement I will give a
brief description to illustrate the working relation
which evolved in a voluntary organization composed
of both Christians and non-Christians.

Jimmie Yen had not proceeded far in his campaigns to eliminate illiteracy before the demand for
his services all over China, Manchuria, and Mongolia
was simply overwhelming. The work in the rural districts brought him face to face with the realization
that the whole question of rural reconstruction was
basic in China's adjustment to the new day. He was
urged time and again to join the government and
incorporate his work with the national educational
system. He felt that under the conditions existing at
the time, this would imperil the whole undertaking.
It was much better for his organization to work at

the problem free from government restrictions, and let the government profit by the lessons which he and his colleagues were able to work out. A National Committee composed of leading educators and other prominent citizens was organized. This Committee took on the responsibility of promoting the enterprise throughout China. Ting Hsien, a provincial district near Peiping (formerly Peking), was selected as an experiment station both for mass education and rural reconstruction. Ting Hsien had a population of four hundred thousand and an area of nearly four hundred and eighty square miles, with four hundred and seventy-two villages. There were 1,909 other districts in China where life is similar to that in Ting Hsien.

Since 1926 Yen and a group of able, devoted, and highly trained colleagues have been giving themselves to working out in the most thorough and systematic way all the problems of this one district. Practically every member of his staff has taken advanced studies in the United States or in Europe, or in both places. They have all had highly attractive offers in the way of position and financial remuneration, which they have invariably turned down. They are a brotherhood joined in a great sacrifice which they consider a great privilege.

Mr. Edgar Snow, who visited Ting Hsien in 1933, gives us a recent account of Yen's enterprise: "Wherein is Ting Hsien different? Wherein lies its significance? How is it possible that change, even if

vast change in Ting Hsien, which is but a single cell
in the tissue of China, may eventually alter the whole
organism? What is it like today, this 'Tranquil
County' which, like other *hsien* in China, has been
abused, looted, flooded with opium and heroin,
heavily overtaxed, but seldom taught or understood
by the various republican governments of our day?

"Outwardly it looks much like any other grouping
of villages in China. The differences wrought are
in people, in their psychology, in their whole outlook
on life—not in the belching smokestacks of imported
foreign industry.

"Over there on a farm stands a family gazing
intently at the yellow earth, where a square of it has
been smoothed over. A young man, using his hoe
handle for a stylus, practices characters: 'Wipe out
illiteracy in China!' he laboriously writes. And then
another, a young girl, takes the hoe and proudly in-
scribes, 'Build new citizens for the nation!' Perhaps
the old man writes also, and the old woman."

Mr. Snow describes two hundred young farmers
happily leveling and grading the road, youths who
have come from six different villages. He describes
the wheelbarrow hospital, the groups listening to the
radio, a radio made in Ting Hsien and owned by the
village. At another place, by looking over a mud
wall he sees forty or more young girls in an impro-
vised schoolroom. He tells of farmers who have introduced goats, Rhode Island Reds, Poland-China

hogs, and overhears them using such words as "research," "experiment," and "scientific."

"Where," he asks, "is the spark center from which these innovations generate? It is in the four hundred and fifteen schools in Ting Hsien's four hundred and seventy-two villages—mass educational schools, run almost entirely by the people, without government support. Here thousands of young men and women have learned to read and write. Here, which is more, thousands of them have learned, are learning now, to work together, plan together, organize themselves into formidable farmers' unions, joining other village units, striving for social, economic, and political betterment. . . .

"But the Ting Hsien project is a much more extensive enterprise than the mere spreading of literacy. People had to be taught what to do with literacy. They found that it was necessary to reorganize and rebuild in every department of life, to remake its very fabric. With the failure of attempts to superimpose half a dozen alien social and political systems on China from above, they concluded that the people could be regenerated only from the bottom, never from the top. And the new growths must be something rooted in China but nourished by modern scientific knowledge. So at Ting Hsien men sought the bottom."[1]

If China is to be made a Christian nation, there

[1] "Awakening the Masses in China," by Edgar Snow, *New York Herald Tribune* Magazine Section, Sunday, December 17, 1933.

must be a great deal of work similar to what Yen and his colleagues are doing at Ting Hsien. There they see the need not only to preach the principles of Jesus, but to spell them out in the merest villages in terms of daily life—to spell them out for the ignorant, the poor, the exploited; and these highly trained experts do this willingly at great personal sacrifice.

What Yen and his colleagues are doing is in the last analysis a most common sense piece of reform. But to most people, accustomed to thinking of reform as an occasional function of government, reform does not usually seem to connote a remodeling from the very foundations of a society. Yet this is what is happening at Ting Hsien, where the highest has come to teach the lowliest and where the lowliest has responded without reserve. These extraordinarily able men have conceived it to be their duty as Christians to go and live on equal terms with the poorest peasants, and there to grapple with some of the most perplexing problems of a Confucian society. They have brought with them a wealth of experience and training which they voluntarily place at the service of all, Confucian, Buddhist, and Taoist alike. Thus this practicing of the teachings of Christ in their daily lives reaches proportions difficult to exaggerate; yet it has arisen in spirits self-dedicated to deeds, not to words, for the lasting benefit of the whole land. Out of it has grown between the peasant farmers and these Christian scholars a harmony of effort and a singleness of purpose that is imbued with Christian faith and hope and love. The utter lack of self-consciousness in matters of religious belief and the attendant willingness of all to coöperate for the sake of all have provided object-lessons which have revealed to me new and effective methods of the Christians' approach to the Chinese.

Chapter XII: One Sows, Another Reaps

THE first meeting of the World's Student Christian Federation to be held outside of Europe or America met in Tokyo during the spring of 1907. The welcome extended to the visiting delegates by Japan was extraordinary. As a special courtesy, the Imperial Gardens were thrown open for a reception to them. Baron Goto, whose able administration of Formosa had attracted the attention of all Japan, was host to the visitors at a garden party in his own spacious grounds, famous for their beauty at cherry-blossom time. Baron and Baroness Goto received the delegates in their cherry grove. Although it was too cold for the cherry blossoms, *the immense trees were in full bloom*! The delegates were enchanted by the beauty of the scene. Later I learned that Baron Goto was so eager for his guests to carry away a memory of Japan in cherry-blossom season that he employed a host of decorators—one thousand, I was told—to decorate the great cherry trees in his garden. The blossoms had been made by hand and tied to the trees. The effect was perfect.

Hospitality in Japan has been developed into a fine art, so perfected through centuries of practice

that it comes as a revelation to her visitors. These
assurances of welcome and the provisions made for
the pleasure of the Federation delegates were deeply
appreciated. Even more impressive was the solicitude, manifested particularly by the educational authorities, by Baron Goto, Viscount Shibusawa, and
Count Okuma, to afford the convention all possible
help in accomplishing its purpose. Auditoriums were
made available for mass meetings of students, both
Japanese and Chinese. The necessary adjustments
in schedules were arranged to enable students to attend the Federation meetings. With the great numbers of Chinese students then in the city, Tokyo had
become the largest student center in the world. In
the meetings for Japanese students the attendance
and interest compared favorably with that at similar
Federation gatherings in Europe and America. But
the response on the part of the Chinese students was
extraordinary. This was doubtless due in no small
measure to C. T. Wang's meetings, which had continued for so long with unabated interest. But the
situation was also an index of the renaissance
throughout China. John R. Mott and Sherwood
Eddy were the speakers of the convention most in
demand at mass meetings among the Chinese students in Tokyo. The interest manifested by them
encouraged me to believe that the students in the
government colleges of China might respond in a
similar manner.

Consequently, toward the close of the Federation

convention I asked Eddy whether he could not be
released from his work in India for an evangelistic
tour of the government colleges in China. I found
him reluctant to consent to an extended absence from
his work among the Indian students. Finally I said,
"If you will come to China for three months I
will guarantee you an average attendance of a thousand students at every meeting you hold." There-
upon he agreed to come in the spring of the following
year.

Arrangements were made for his tour to begin in
Hongkong, since this was the first port he would
touch. It was not the ideal place in which to inaugurate his campaign, as the colony was not an outstanding student center: Hongkong University had
not then been founded. In preliminary correspondence with the Christian leaders of Hongkong I
stressed the importance, from the standpoint of
Eddy's whole tour, of having the first center give a
demonstration of the possibilities in an Eddy visit.
I urged large faith and thorough planning in making
preparations for the meetings. When I reached
Hongkong some days before Eddy's ship was to ar-
rive, I found that the auditorium selected for the
first meeting was a church far from the center of the
colony and with a seating capacity of less than three
hundred.

"If the meeting is a success," the committee explained, "we will move the second night to larger

quarters. After the people are assured that Doctor Eddy can make good, we can increase the audiences."

"Why not begin with the City Hall?" I inquired. "It is located in the heart of the colony, will seat twelve hundred and will give distinction to the undertaking."

"The cost is prohibitive," replied one of the committee, "several hundred dollars for the first night, and probably a thousand for the series of meetings. Moreover, with an unknown speaker how can we expect to fill such a large place?"

I did all that I could to strengthen their faith and challenged them with the fact that a special responsibility rested upon Hongkong, the first city on Eddy's itinerary to set the pace for his tour throughout China. After thorough and lengthy deliberation a unanimous decision was reached, and a committee was appointed to proceed at once to rent the City Hall. Eddy's coming was heralded in the city papers and tickets were mailed to the most likely prospects. With the day for the opening meeting came a storm —and in those days a rain in China was considered sufficient cause to stop even a battle, but to the surprise of us all the City Hall was crowded to its full capacity. The meetings in Hongkong grew in power throughout the series and did indeed set a high standard for the rest of the tour.

In every center Eddy was received with enthusiasm and the interest deepened with his stay. The tour removed all doubt as to Eddy's appeal to the

student class, which included the old intelligentsia as
well as the students in modern colleges. But the
series of meetings was as instructive in its failure as
in its success. The failure, to be sure, was not due
to Sherwood Eddy, but to our overemphasis upon
securing attendance at the meetings rather than upon
the more important task of harvesting their results.
In each city visited by Eddy there were large numbers of inquirers from among the Confucianists. In
order to prepare them for an intelligent declaration
of Christian faith it was necessary to provide them
with from four to six months' instruction. The number of inquirers was so large that the churches were
overwhelmed with the demand for competent teachers, and consequently many of the inquirers were
not enrolled in classes.

At the close of Eddy's visit he was asked—and
agreed—to return for another tour in which the mis-
takes made in planning the first tour would be
corrected. To this end Dr. W. E. Taylor of Shanghai agreed to give one year in making preliminary
arrangements for this second visit of Eddy, and another year to conserving its results. The time selected for Eddy's return to China, 1913, most
fortunately coincided with a visit of Mott as chairman of the International Missionary Council, who
agreed to reserve a portion of his time for the
evangelistic undertaking and a joint tour with Eddy.
In his preparations Doctor Taylor visited every

center at which meetings were to be held. The co-
operation of all Christian workers was secured, sometimes at the cost of radical readjustment of their
plans. Leaders, lay and clerical, definitely arranged
their schedules to allow time to conduct classes for
inquirers following the meetings. Many workers took
thorough courses of training in preparation for that
task.

Doctor Taylor also secured the coöperation of the
educational authorities and government officials in
each city. Arrangements were perfected for providing large auditoriums. Parliament buildings, city
halls and theaters were secured or, wherever necessary, large temporary auditoriums were erected;
these consisted of a framework of bamboo poles and
roof and walls of palm leaves or reed matting—a
method of construction well-known in China. In some
cities arrangements were made for C. H. Robertson
to precede the evangelistic speaker with a week of
his scientific lectures at which the coming meetings
would be advertised. Doctor Taylor proved a master
in attention to such detail and in such comprehensive planning.

The tour, as finally arranged, included China,
Japan, Korea, and Manchuria. The meetings were
designed primarily for the intelligentsia. Admission
was by ticket and the tickets were carefully distributed to selected groups. Arrangements were made
to have news reports of the meetings in the daily
press, followed by carefully prepared articles on

Christianity. More than a hundred newspapers co-operated in this arrangement. The whole schedule went through according to plan and our most optimistic expectations were exceeded.

In Foochow, Eddy's last center, the attendance was five thousand a day for six days. The Chamber of Commerce attended in a body, and at one meeting the members of seventy-two reform societies were present. The Provincial Parliament which was in session at the time adjourned to have Eddy address them. Thirteen government colleges postponed examinations and closed their doors in order that the students might attend the meetings. So great was the demand for teachers of Bible classes for the seventeen hundred inquirers that it became necessary for a number of months to exclude from membership in these classes for new converts all Foochow people who had previously become Christians.

I had joined Mott in Singapore and accompanied him throughout his stay in China. At Canton, our first stop, Mott's opening evangelistic meeting was to be held in a recently erected modern theater with a seating capacity of three thousand. The committee in charge of the meetings had issued five thousand tickets, largely to government-school students. I suggested to Mott that we get to the theater early: I was fearful that the first night's audience might seem lost in such an immense place and wanted Mott to become adjusted to conditions before he began his address. We reached the theater a half or three-

quarters of an hour ahead of time and found a great
crowd of students milling around the door and a
group of policemen on hand. One of them courteously
explained that we could not be admitted, that the
theater was filled to the last seat and the doors were
locked. I introduced Mott, and the doors were opened
just enough to give us admittance. We were taken
to the stage, where about twenty of the leading
officials of the province were seated. They were introduced to Mott by the Commissioner of Foreign
Affairs. The large theater with its four galleries was
filled with students dressed in the typical simple gray
uniforms with collars of their jackets buttoned
tightly at the neck. Mott spoke to his audience for an
hour and a half. In his address there was no appeal
to the emotions, no recourse to stories or incidents
to add interest. It was severely logical, straightforward, convincing, and made dynamic by the fire of
Mott's own conviction. He finished and took his seat
on the platform. From the topmost gallery to the
stage there was not a stir. After a considerable pause
Mott asked the chairman what it meant.

"They want another address," replied the chairman.

He spoke again for nearly an hour, and even then
the audience was dismissed with some difficulty. This
great interest in Canton did not prove to be exceptional. Quite the reverse was true.

Mott's evangelistic meetings had to be adjusted
to his other engagements in China and Japan. These

seemed to demand our declining an invitation to hold meetings for the students of Mukden, as he passed through on his way to Japan. But when we reached Peking the petitions and protests from Mukden were overwhelming. Dr. John Ross, the great Scotch missionary, and his fellow-workers were insistent. The Governor offered to build and equip an auditorium, and the Minister of Education and presidents of the government colleges proffered their cooperation. Sunday, which I had been guarding as a day of greatly needed rest for Mott, was the only day available. When we reached Mukden we were able to realize to some measure the Governor's expectations by the size of the auditorium which he had caused to be erected. It seated five thousand, but proved too small for the number of students and older intelligentsia who asked admittance long before ten o'clock, the announced time for the opening.

The meeting lasted three hours or more. As it was to be his only address to the students, Mott broke his rule and asked for inquirers at a first meeting. To my amazement the Minister of Education, who was chairman of the meeting, arose and reinforced Mott's plea for the students to make definite decisions as to the claims of Jesus Christ upon their own lives. He urged them to join Bible classes with a view to learning Jesus' way of life.

In their joint effort in China Mott and Eddy, either together or separately, conducted meetings in thirteen great cities. As the tour progressed the at tendance at meetings increased and the response to their message became more marked, reaching the climax with Eddy at Foochow and with Mott at Mukden, the last cities visited.

Eddy planned to return to China the following year for a third tour. It was, as I recall, while he and I were crossing the Pacific after the close of that third series of evangelistic meetings that Eddy gave me the philosophy of his approach to Oriental students.

"I worked it out," he explained, "as a result of blunders I made in my early contacts with Hindu students in India. I would allow myself to be led into a denunciation of Hinduism, or, what was almost as bad, into an attempt to prove the superiority of Christianity. The Indians are skilled in dialectics and I often got the worst of the argument. But I soon found that even if I got the best of the argument, I lost my man."

He finally came to see that there were four courses open to him in dealing with non-Christians: wholesale condemnation, wholesale commendation, comparison or contrast, and "completion" in the sense that Jesus meant when he declared, "I came not to destroy, but to fulfill."

In his rapid succinct style he then gave me these convictions: "To condemn the other man's religion is to repel him. To commend it with unstinted praise leaves him self-satisfied. To contrast the two religions, endeavoring to prove that we have a better religion than he, throws him on the defensive—the worst possible attitude for receiving the truth." This statement of his convictions explained to me his strict adherence to the fourth course.

In the first half of 1914, the time of Eddy's third tour in China, the country was in an especially favorable mood for the reception of his message. The conservatism of the old Manchu régime was dead and all classes were irrevocably committed to making China a modern nation. While the Republic was indisputably recognized and accepted, the few months since its establishment gave unmistakable signs that it could not be counted upon to solve all the nation's problems. The widespread illiteracy among the masses was proving an unstable base for democratic control. The more discerning persons were detecting that President Yüan Shih-k'ai was giving but lip service to the republican ideals. Although sobered by these conditions, the leaders of the nation had not yet been disillusioned by the World War as to the moral superiority of Western civilization. Nor had they any premonition of the life-and-death struggle with atheistic communism which was to follow; so that Eddy's reception on his third tour was little short of an ovation.

Much of the success of this visit was due to C. T. Wang and C. L. Nieh, who acted as his interpreters. Wang, after returning from his four years in

America, was called from one high government post
to another, much as were Hamilton and Jefferson
in the early days of the American Republic. His integrity, boldness, and eloquence had made him the
idol of the students. He had just resigned from a
position in Yüan Shih-k'ai's cabinet over an issue in
which he, rather than the President, had the approval of the people.

Wang's high standing is indicated by a story cir-
culated widely at the time. A friend was said to have
inquired of the President, "Why did you accept the
resignation of a man whose widespread popularity
gave such strength to the administration?"

The President replied, "I recognized the loss to my
government. But I could not buy him and I could not
scare him. What could I do with a man like that?"

One might well ask, if Wang could serve as an
interpreter, why have Eddy? Wang himself was a
great evangelist, and as a popular hero of the revolution he could command as large an audience as
Eddy. Why did the Chinese Christian leaders—and
Wang himself—think the combination of Eddy and
Wang better than Wang alone? Interpretation seems
a most awkward and unsatisfactory way to present
an appeal. But there can be no doubt that Eddy
and Wang together made a more powerful appeal
than either of them would have made alone. The complete fellowship between the two men seemed a symbol of potential fellowship between Orient and Occi-

dent—a synthesis deeply moving, convincing, and prophetic of ultimate world unity.

C. L. Nieh could trace his lineage back some centuries before the time of Confucius. One of his ancestors was the most famous disciple of the great sage. And Tsêng Kuo-fan, Nieh's grandfather, had rescued the Empire from the T'ai P'ing Rebellion and was considered China's greatest man of the nineteenth century. The family ranked in prominence next to that of Confucius. Through the influence of Dr. and Mrs. Edward H. Hume, in whose home he was a frequent visitor, Nieh became a Christian. Although he had been baptized but a few months before Eddy came to Changsha, he accepted the heavy responsibility of interpretation for the evangelist during the meetings in that city. It was a task involving the use of a vocabulary and an acquaintance with Christianity which gave Nieh many misgivings. But he was a great success, as revealed in his eloquence, passion, and prestige, and in his accurate conveyance of the Christian teaching. His Confucian background had been a preparation for the difficult and important service into which he was called so soon after becoming a Christian.

This third tour was conspicuous in the recognition accorded Eddy by the highest officials. Yüan Shih-k'ai, the President, early conferred with him and showed genuine interest in what he was to do. The Vice-President, Li Yüan-hung, arranged a meeting in his own home, where he asked Eddy to address the members of his family and a circle of close friends on Christianity. While the Vice-President never joined the Church, he revealed during the rest of his life abundant proof of being a convinced Christian.

Hangchow, at one time the national capital, beautiful, proud, and a seat of Confucian culture, had manifested slight interest in Eddy's first and second tours. But at the time of the third tour the attitude of the city had radically changed. The Governor was a young man in his thirties who had already distinguished himself by his political and moral reforms. The next ranking official, the Commissioner of Foreign Affairs, was S. T. Wen, who came from a family which had furnished many officials to the country. He was tall and alert, idealistic, and possessed of a charming manner. C. T. Wang was a native of the province of Chêkiang, of which Hangchow was the capital, and its most distinguished citizen. The Governor and the Commissioner of Foreign Affairs pressed the invitation for Eddy and Wang to go to Hangchow, and threw themselves whole-heartedly into the plans to make the visit a success. At a meeting arranged by the Governor for Eddy and Wang to meet and address the officials, Mr. Wen was converted. Within a week he joined the Church and at the risk of his official position allied himself with all Christian activities. As part of the plan for conserving the results of the meetings, a large Bible class made up entirely of scholars and men of distinction in the city was organized under the able and devoted leadership of Zia Hong-lai, the leading Christian author of the country. Within a year of this visit of Eddy to Hangchow the attitude of the whole city toward Christianity had so completely changed that the interest of the people, high and low, led them to active participation in a wide variety of Christian enterprises.

Some months afterwards I wrote down the factors, apart from Eddy's own work, which had contributed to the outcome of the meetings at Hangchow. The following seemed clear to me: first, the favoring conditions in the country; second, the whole-hearted co-operation of the two leading officials of the province; third, the masterly interpretation and the prestige of C. T. Wang; fourth, the service of Zia Hong-lai, that ripe Confucian scholar and the Chinese Christian who had most deeply studied the relation between Confucianism and Christianity; and fifth, the presence in Hangchow of a small group of missionaries who were in close touch with leading Chinese and who had both a real understanding of Chinese civilization and exceptional ability in the language. All the factors in bringing about the results in Hangchow were constructively related to the Confucian background of the people and seemed marvelously assembled and fitted into the peculiar conditions of that particular situation. It must be, I felt, the work of God. But it was clear that God had not worked by magic. If God had prepared Eddy, Wang, and Zia, had he not also prepared the Governor and the Commissioner of Foreign Affairs? A few weeks later Eddy and Wang were at Nanking. In the middle of the campaign Eddy's throat failed him and Commissioner Wen, the Hangchow Christian of less than a month's standing, joined Wang and spoke with great power.

Eddy's tour revealed an amazing eagerness on the part of China's leaders to face the claims of Christianity. I know of no Christian country where he could have commanded equally influential coöperation or found such deep interest in his message. Officials and educators of distinction definitely decided to become Christians and allied themselves with the Church. Chambers of commerce held special meetings to hear him speak. The governors of provinces repeatedly called all their officials together to have him address them on religion. In one capital city the local committee decided to hold a series of meetings throughout the province led by those who had heard Eddy, and thus extend the range of his mission. In aid of the plan the Governor sent a letter to each magistrate of the twelve cities of the province, announcing the speakers and dates of the evangelistic meetings and requesting all officials to coöperate. In the same city at a banquet given to Eddy by the Minister of Education and a group of nearly fifty educators, one of the speakers said, "Confucianism alone cannot save China. We need the moral dynamic and principle of progress which Christianity can give." This statement voiced the mind of a large proportion of the responsible leaders of China at that time.

In a meeting for inquirers in Peking, Eddy recognized one former governor, two generals, a private secretary to President Yüan Shih-k'ai, the director of China's national bank, prominent officials, and a young non-Christian philanthropist.

Amoy, a rich and important but comparatively small city, erected in an open square a temporary auditorium for Eddy's meetings with a seating capacity of five thousand. The demand for tickets was so great that they were not distributed, but were placed in the Y. M. C. A., where eight thousand men came in person and wrote out applications for tickets.

The wide social reach of Eddy's work was illustrated by two incidents which happened in the city of Amoy. With admittance by ticket only, the committee hoped to confine the attendance to the educated class. At one end of the social scale was the Mayor of the city, who made a clear-cut decision to become a Christian. At the other end was Ling Po, leader of a notorious gang of bandits, who had come down from the mountains to the city. After vain attempts to secure a ticket, he cut a hole in the frail wall of the auditorium large enough to let him peep in and listen. Later by some means he procured a ticket and gained admittance to the meeting.

As a climax to his denunciation of the well-known corruption in official circles Eddy cried out, "The robbers must stop robbing China." Ling Po applied the words to himself and was deeply convicted of his sins. When Eddy called for those who wanted to denounce their sins and enter a new way of life, to stand and give their names for Bible classes, Ling Po, although there was a price of a thousand dollars on his head, arose, gave his name, and asked some one to sign a card for him.

Since I began writing this chapter I have received a letter from Eddy written as he was completing his ninth tour in China. He tells of his visit to Amoy, sixteen years after the visit referred to above, and speaks of the Mayor who, he says, "has been standing like a rock or tower of strength as an honest, efficient official and an earnest Christian all these years." He also tells of the former gambler, opium-smoker, and bandit, Ling Po. "He has lived all these years," Eddy writes, "as a humble evangelist on ten dollars a month, which he raises himself. He has won over a hundred and seventy of the bandits and their neighbors to the Christian life. In two villages some thirty robbers have given up their hereditary predatory occupation and settled down to farming. This former bandit spoke with tremendous power in three of our meetings this year. I placed his little son in school, and the father has now gone back to the bandits' most dangerous lair in the mountains to win over more of them to this new revolutionary way of life, with its religious, economic, and social implications."

In the spring of 1935 Eddy returned from the trip to which I have just referred. I have learned from my Chinese friends and missionaries that the results of his last series of meetings are more encouraging than those of any previous visit. When one takes into account the present adverse economic and political conditions in China, this response to Eddy's message has especial significance.

I wish to make it clear that it has not been my purpose in this chapter to give an adequate account or an appraisal of the series of nation-wide evangelistic meetings which have been conducted in China during the past twenty-six years. I have attempted only to show their influence in determining my conception of the relation between Christianity and China's moral and religious heritage. I began my religious work in China with the assumption that a recognition of values in the religion of the Chinese was disloyal to Christianity. My intimate association with these evangelistic undertakings has been an important influence in persuading me that my theory was wrong. The great evangelists who took part in the campaigns, such as C. T. Wang, C. Y. Cheng, David Yui, Eddy, Mott, and Stanley Jones, were all men of undoubted loyalty to Jesus Christ, men who depended upon prayer, and men whose beauty of character commanded my highest admira-

tion. The results of their labors have surpassed all
my dreams of what could be done in even a century
of such effort. The meetings have spanned a sufficient period of time in which to test their permanent
worth. The response, while dependent in a measure
upon the conditions in the country and hence more
marked at some periods than at others, has been
notable in season and out. The evangelistic meetings
have immeasurably strengthened the influence of
Christianity upon the intelligentsia and have quick-
ened the Church's sense of mission to the poor and
oppressed. They have been a great force in uniting
all denominations into an effective national unity.

These meetings centered the attention of all upon
there being a way of life not merely for the individual, but also for the nation. And therein lies their
broadest significance. These Christians were made
without emotional hysteria and with a high sense of
personal dedication to the task of shaping a nation's
destiny.

All these considerations led me to the discovery
of vast resources for good in the Chinese non-Christian community where in my early days I had supposed an implacable foe existed. I marveled at the
tremendous response to these meetings, and still
more at the results which followed from them and
spread throughout the land. "How," I asked, "could
I account for such great faith in a non-Christian
land?" Then I remembered Christ's experience when,

on his return to Capernaum, he was accosted by the
Roman centurion seeking help.

"Sir, my servant is lying ill at home with paraly-
sis, in terrible agony."

Jesus replied, "I will come and heal him."

The centurion protested, "Sir, I am not fit to have
you under my roof; only say the word, and my servant will be cured."

When Jesus heard this, he marveled and said,
"I have never met faith like this anywhere in Israel."

Jesus then said unto the centurion, "Go; as you
have had faith, your prayer is granted."[1]

How naturally Jesus accepted the faith of the
centurion. It was just as I should have expected Dr.
Timothy Richard to accept the faith of a Confucianist. The training of a Confucianist would certainly prepare a person for an understanding of
Jesus as well as would the training of a Roman
centurion. Why should I have misgivings about the
faith of the Confucianists who wanted to see China
saved and thought that Jesus could help? I could
interpret neither Jesus' act nor his words as a tearing
up, root and branch, of the centurion's faith.

I had gone to China with the idea that my work
was to sow, but the words, "I sent you to reap," kept
ringing in my ears; "to reap a crop for which you
did not toil; other men have toiled, and you reap
the profit of their toil."[2]

[1] Matthew 8:6-13. From *A New Translation of the Bible*, by
James Moffatt, Harper & Brothers.

[2] *Ibid.*, John 4:38.

"I am rich!" I exclaimed. "I have come into a great inheritance. My wealth has been gathering for thousands of years. Confucius, Mencius, Mo Ti, Buddha, Abraham, Moses, Isaiah, Paul, Jesus—I have entered into their inheritance. I am heir of the ages. I am sent not to dig up the roots, but to gather in the harvest."

As a result of this discovery I was able to account for the great audiences of older literati and government-college students who crowded with such eagerness into the evangelistic meetings: C. T. Wang, David Yui, Mott, and Eddy were gathering the harvest of seed sown long ago. Harvest-time in all ages and among all people is, I reflected, a time of joy. I had left America for China with the thought that I was making a great personal sacrifice, and behold, here I was to spend all my days in a harvest festival!

Chapter *XIII:* I Take My Bearings

COÖPERATION with the Confucianists had developed so rapidly that it had assumed large proportions before I became aware of how far apart had grown my practice and my original philosophy of missionary work. True, each piece of work carried on in coöperation with the Confucianists had been carefully considered before its adoption. To safeguard its Christian basis, each directing committee was composed entirely of Christians, and the program included Bible classes and evangelistic meetings. The Confucianists offered no restraint to a straightforward presentation of the Christian message or appeal. But I knew the conflict between my theory and my practice must be reckoned with if I were to have peace of mind. I determined to make a restudy of the Bible against the background of my Far Eastern experience. For lack of any other time this plan was carried out for the most part when traveling on steamboats, in railway coaches, sedan chairs, or Peking carts.

Although I expected to get more help from the New Testament than the Old, I realized that it was the Old Testament which had first implanted in my mind the fighting attitude toward the non-Christian religions. In our home on the Georgia plantation it had been our custom to read the chapters of the Bible consecutively from Genesis through the Revelation. During the long winter evenings my brother and I would sit in front of the great fireplace beside our mother and read the fiery denunciations of the Israelites who went whoring after other gods. She would reinforce the words of the prophets with the story of her father, a Methodist preacher in Virginia, who had considered it as important to turn out the unworthy from the church as to bring in new members. The great personalities of the Old Testament had appealed to my youthful imagination more than those in the New Testament; Abraham, Moses, Samuel, and David were vivid and living persons. Those who most influenced my thought with reference to my missionary work were Elijah, Amos, Isaiah, and Ezra.

The most valuable lesson from the study of Elijah came as a surprise which, I must confess, startled me. I had been picturing myself as Elijah, and the Confucianists as the prophets of Baal. But in reality Elijah was a native and the prophets of Baal were the foreign missionaries. The prophets of Baal were not only the representatives of a foreign religion, but also the instruments of political intrigue, introduced through the powerful influence of the queen, the able, resolute and unscrupulous daughter of the Tyrian king. Elijah was a Hebrew living in his own country and defending both the national integrity and the religious inheritance of Israel. The worship of Baal with its horde of Tyrian priests threatened the destruction of the very warp and woof of Hebrew civilization. Elijah saw this clearly and fought with desperate courage to preserve what was more precious than life itself. He was fighting both as a patriot and as a religious zealot.

I then tried to imagine a Confucianist reading the story of Elijah's life. He would put himself in the place of Elijah. The nations which were planning to divide China among themselves, which had forced opium upon China, which had compelled China to abrogate her sovereignty by a series of unequal treaties signed in front of loaded cannons—these nations were filling China with their missionaries to teach the "heathen" Chinese the way of peace. As Elijah recognized in Jezebel and her religious propaganda the ruin of his country, the Confucianist might easily see in the missionaries the spearhead of the forces for the destruction of China's civilization.

I remembered with chagrin how much there was in the missionary propaganda to confirm the Confucianist in this point of view. Passages from missionary addresses came to my mind:

"Why should we expend our resources for missions? . . . It is a fight for life. We have got to conquer them or they will conquer us."

"Commodore Perry knocked at the sea gates of Japan, and in the name of a Christian republic de-

manded entrance. . . . In 1858, the great breach
was made in the Chinese wall, and by the treaty of
Tientsin one-third of the human race were made accessible to Christian nations; . . . that wide door
was opened, not by the vermilion pencil of the Emperor, but by the decree of the Eternal."[1]

I recalled my visit to Peking on the first anniversary of the Relief of the Legations and the revelation which it gave me of the nameless outrages upon
innocent Chinese by the armies of the Western
nations.

There came to my mind an experience which I had
some months before on a visit to Hangchow. The
principal of a noted school for boys in the city, a
man of deep learning and winsome personality, had
become interested in Christianity at one of Sherwood Eddy's meetings and afterwards had joined
the Bible class for members of the literati conducted
by Zia Hong-lai. The principal professed Christianity and was exerting a strong Christian influence in
both his school and the community. One of the missionaries of Hangchow asked me to spend Sunday
morning with the principal in an effort to induce him
to join the Church. It was a memorable experience.
We had the whole morning together. It was easy to
talk with him about the deepest things in life. I spoke
to him about joining the Church, and reminded him
how greatly it stood in need of his help. He bore
testimony to his loyalty to Jesus Christ, but he said,

[1] See quotations in Chapter II.

"When I think of joining the Church I cannot disassociate it from all the wrongs which have been heaped upon China. It is like asking me to identify myself with everything I hate."

I shall never forget his very words, "everything I hate." He was so gentle, kindly, lovable, it came as a shock to me that he was capable of hate. He had received a psychic injury which would require years to heal.

The more I contemplated the mood of a Confucian Elijah, the less confidence I had in an antagonistic approach to him. It was evident that I must disassociate my message from the assaults made by the so-called Christian countries upon China's national integrity. Somehow I must make the Chinese feel that I was not an enemy, but a friend to the most prized elements in their civilization.

From Elijah I proceeded to a study of Isaiah, Amos, the prophets of the Exile, the prophets of the post-exilic period, and some of the Messianic Psalms. Out of the sorrow and blasted hopes caused by the threatened, and finally by the accomplished, destruction of the kingdoms of Samaria and Judah, these inspired leaders came to see the glory and grandeur of Israel's mission to the world. China's then threatened dismemberment gave poignant interest to the study of this literature, unsurpassed in beauty of expression and in depth of insight.

I was impressed with the fact that in choosing a race and nation through whom he could give a special revelation of himself, God did not select a people on some island isolated from all heathen ideas, laws, customs, and institutions. He did not select a people sheltered from enemies. He chose a group of nomads without a country, without prestige, wealth, or power. They gained a precarious foothold in the highlands of Palestine, but never eliminated the heathen Canaanites, their kinsmen. They were surrounded by Egyptians, Babylonians, Assyrians, Phœnicians, Syrians, and Canaanites. Their whole life was intermingled with that of peoples of greater strength and influence and with a civilization older than their own. They had to carry their spark of light through the storm of rain and wind. In spite of it all—in a measure because of it all—they prepared the way for a universal religion.

On the other hand, the study made me see that the danger of syncretism was vivid and real. Several times the distinctive religion of Israel seemed almost overwhelmed; even the priests, who were the teachers of the people, countenanced pagan practices until the worship of Jehovah became debased. The great prophets were forced to carry on a continuous fight to prevent apostasy.

The young Christian Church in China was surrounded by conditions which, in some important respects, were similar to those in which Israel had been engulfed. In the midst of an environment so alien and so powerful, it would be folly to disregard the dangers which have faced the small Chinese Church even from the beginning.

In the seventh century the Nestorian Church had begun missionary work in China, and had been at one time probably larger than the Chinese Christian Church at the time of my restudy of the Bible. Yet practically the only traces left of Nestorianism were a stone tablet which had been erected at Ch'angan in 781, three imperial edicts, a "Hymn in Praise of the Holy Trinity," and a few old documents. The Christian Church should now be constantly on its guard against a like reassimilation. On the other hand, I realized that an undiscriminating fear of syncretism might retard some of the most distinctive and important functions of Christianity and might obscure some of its most vital characteristics, for example, its powers of appropriation and synthesis.

In China idolatry was predominant among Taoists and Buddhists. The Confucianists were opposed to it, as indicated in the classics and in the quotations which I have given from the *Sacred Edict*. The Christian Church should be kept free from idolatry. But that was not one of the live questions in China, and the missionary could well leave its abolishment to the Chinese themselves.

The most likely door through which syncretism might enter was ancestor worship, and the missionaries had already found they could wisely leave this question also to the Chinese Christians. The missionaries could expend all their energies, declare all their truth, show all their devotion, in a constructive program. Confucianism is a system of ethics rather than a religion; the attitude to assume toward it would be to commend its ethics and to *furnish the dynamic*, an essential element which was lacking and for which Confucian leaders were themselves eagerly hunting.

The way for Christians to keep from falling into the false doctrines of non-Christian faiths was to maintain a close relationship with God. The Christians should not isolate themselves; rather they should get into the stream of national life to direct the course which their country must take in this new day. They must see that, as individuals and as Christians, they are obligated to throw the weight of their influence into the balance for the good of their country in a time of national peril.

I remembered the keen awareness with which I had perceived, at various times, the peril so imminent to China's national integrity; and I recalled, too, the apparent complacency with which the Chinese themselves seemed to view this constant threat to their country's welfare. It was several years before I began to understand what was really passing through the minds of the Chinese. "What is the matter with the Chinese?" I would ask with no little petulance. "Why do they not wake up? Do they not realize that they are hopelessly behind the times in everything—education, government, industry, and religion?" Gradually I came to comprehend that the Chinese realized their civilization was in danger of disintegration; they were resisting each change in order to hold back the flood which threatened to change everything.

Many of the Chinese leaders had grave misgivings as to the ability of the country to make adequate adjustment of labor conditions if there should be a speedy introduction of machinery. There was much to make them hesitate—the overthrow of the old examination system, which supplied the country with trained officials, before time had elapsed in which to educate the people in the selection of their officials by vote; the radical change in China's most fundamental institution, the family system; the dependence upon force rather than upon justice in settling international questions. These with many other probable consequences of becoming "modern" made them pause before abandoning their civilization, one which had enjoyed the longest continuous existence of any in human history and which had enriched the world with priceless contributions to art, peace, philosophy, and literature.

I came slowly to understand that for a nation to change its civilization is an adventure fraught with difficulty and inevitable peril. A change of government is in comparison a minor matter even if, as in the case of the American Revolution, it means independence. Civilization is the intricate pattern of corporate life, its living threads inextricably interwoven. After many centuries cultural habits are established which are difficult to break. It is much easier to kill a civilization than to bring it to a rebirth. Human history, short as it is, is strewn with the remains of not a few great civilizations. "Would the impact of the West upon China result," I asked myself, "in a disintegration of her civilization, as happened in ancient Egypt, or in a rebirth which would insure her rightful place in the modern world?"

No Chinese during the past twenty years has exerted a greater influence upon Chinese thought than Dr. Hu Shih. Since his student days at Columbia University he has never wavered for a moment in insisting, as though in answer to my question, that China must throw herself whole-heartedly into the stream of modern life. He calls upon her intellectual leaders to emancipate her from the fetters of the past. He hastens, however, to affirm that, "This emancipation cannot be accomplished by any wholesale importation of occidental philosophies alone."[1]

"How can we Chinese," Dr. Hu Shih asks, "feel at ease in this new world which at first sight appears to be so much at variance with what we have long regarded as our own civilization? For it is perfectly natural and justifiable that a nation with a glorious past and with a distinctive civilization of its own making should never feel quite at home in a new civilization, if that new civilization is looked upon as part and parcel imported from alien lands and

[1] Hu Shih, *The Development of the Logical Method in Ancient China*, Introduction p. 8. Kegan Paul, Trench, Trubner & Co., London, 1922.

forced upon it by external necessities of national existence. And it would surely be a great loss to mankind at large if the acceptance of this new civilization should take the form of abrupt displacement instead of organic assimilation, thereby causing the disappearance of the old civilization. The real problem, therefore, may be restated thus: How can we best assimilate modern civilization in such a manner as to make it congenial and congruous and continuous with the civilization of our own making? This larger problem presents itself in every phase of the great conflict between the old civilization and the new. In art, in literature, in politics, and in social life in general, the underlying problem is fundamentally the same."[1]

This essay of Hu Shih's asked precisely the same question that I did as a result of my new study of the Bible and the new interpretation of Chinese civilization which that gave to me. Missionaries had long agreed, I reflected, that Christianity can save China. The question is, "how?" Certainly not in ignoring God's dealing with China in the past by an attempt to dig up, root, stock, and branch, a civilization whose worth had stood the test of four millenniums, but rather by the grafting of all that is noblest in China's inheritance onto our Christian teaching.

That this could be done I now had no doubt. From my experience I had long been aware of the eagerness with which non-Christian Chinese all over the

[1] *Ibid.*, pp. 6-7.

country often went out of their way to lend their support to distinctly Christian activities which they could see had value for the community at large. And I had seen, again, how eagerly they had embraced Christianity and grafted on to it their own native culture. And my study of Paul, as the greatest missionary, more than corroborated what long and varied experience in China had taught me, and what I had at first so unwillingly accepted.

In this study of Paul's life and work I became profoundly impressed with the analogy between two providential sets of preparation: on the one side, the preparation of Paul to deliver his message of love and hope, and that of the Roman Empire to receive it; on the other, the training of missionaries, such as I, to carry that same message, and the long preparation of China to welcome it.

After a thorough tutelage under Gamaliel in the traditional rabbinical schools, a Pharisee of the Pharisees, proud of his race, Paul came at manhood into citizenship in the Roman state; of this fact he took full and proud advantage. He was moreover a citizen of Tarsus, where for years there had existed a famous Greek university. A Jew, reared in the traditional manner and proud of his race, a Roman citizen, and a man closely in touch with Greek culture, Paul had in his background the necessary mingling of racial and cultural influences that make a world-citizen. These positive elements in his preparation would have made him a man of great promise from the beginning of his career, had he not been schooled in a propaganda that "rested on the assumption of the inherent and eternal superiority of one nation and one form of culture over all others."[1] Combined with the arrogance of these assumptions, Paul's natural intensity of spirit made of him a dangerous fanatic who hunted down his fellow nationals for heresy.

His conversion to Christianity, however, worked a complete reversal in his attitude toward those who differed from him in race or religion. The emotional intensity, which had made him a leading persecutor of heretics, now made him almost the antithesis of what he had been. He changed from the separatist, the bigot, the Pharisee, to become the apostle of tolerance, the exemplar of integration. And he felt no conflict in declaring himself both a bond-servant of Jesus and a debtor to the Greek and the Roman, and from his ministry there spread throughout the Empire the leaven of the Gospel.

Integration was the preëminent need of the hour. The civilizations of the Romans, the Greeks, and the Hebrews all had value, indeed high value, but also they had fatal weaknesses. Paul saw and wrought the needed synthesis. In Christianity he had discovered a force which would bind all men together by unbreakable bonds. Here was the solution of the problem which had baffled the Roman Empire. The

[1] C. Harold Dodd, *The Meaning of Paul for Today*, p. 44. London, The Swarthmore Press, 1920.

glory of his mission burst upon him: to build the
divine commonwealth, a kingdom which could never
be destroyed. Those in whose hearts the spirit of
Jesus prevailed could promote no clash of cultures;
in those persons race, nationality, social distinctions,
even distance, were all transcended by such an invisible empire of kindred spirits. Such was Paul's
vision.

In his work, instead of running away from the
great port cities where the civilizations of all the
parts of the Roman Empire mingled, Paul witnessed
in the troubled waters of these centers the breaking
down of old inhibitions; he saw old civilizations suc-
cumb, and a new one spring into life. In the dissolu-
tion of these barriers he found the opportunity for
the new Christian Church.

This study of the Bible against the background of
my missionary experience gradually made the New
Testament a different book to me. I saw it for the
first time as a history of foreign missions. It became
my compendium of missionary policies and methods,
a vade-mecum for every conference. Through Paul's
experience I discovered the tragic inadequacies and
narrowness of the training that I and many of my
colleagues had received, we who had come to China
still steeped in preconceptions and prejudices unre-
lated to reality. The degree of my success as a missionary is in exact proportion to the extent to which
I was able to free myself from these influences, and
to recognize and coöperate with the elements in Chi-

nese civilization friendly to my Christian mission. Thus I came to see that the difficulties attendant upon the cataclysmic changes which had been in progress throughout my twenty-five years in China, really presented an opportunity of the ages. I now perceived that China stands in unprecedented danger, and that it would be a fatal blindness to assume that a threat to the culture of a third of the world's population leaves the remainder unaffected. The Bible had showed me unmistakably the real mission of Christianity to China: it must save the best in her civilization, for this can be integrated into the invisible empire for which Paul labored, the Kingdom of Christ, the only kind of social entity that can save the world.

The present world crisis has sharpened the issue. It is a choice for humanity between a civilization whose god is greed and whose instrument of unification is force, and a civilization whose god is the God of love and whose instrument is the doing of good. Modern science has brought about a physical solidarity. Religion must bring the solidarity of spirit which will make this physical solidarity a living unity. In all the history of mankind the possibility for turning this world into a place of beauty, peace, and plenty, has never been so great, and the possibility of the disintegration of civilization and the destruction of mankind has never seemed more imminent. Under these circumstances the missionary enterprise takes on profoundly new significance. It is

no longer possible for us to have sheltered nooks, isolated nationalities where Christian principles may be
built into a safe and happy world. The destiny of each
nation is intertwined with that of every other. We are
going to be lost together or saved together. We shall
all be prosperous or all be poor, all have peace or
none have peace.

The realization of the need for salvation has been
behind every great religious movement whether
Christian or non-Christian. It is when man sees
that he is in peril of ruin that he is most apt to turn
to God. If Christians have the way of life, if the
way of love is the way out, if the way of the brotherhood of man and the fatherhood of God is the solution of the present world crisis, certainly there has
never been an hour when the compulsion was so great
upon Christians as today. There is no longer need
to make a sharp distinction between the claims of
foreign missions and work at home. When it is possible to talk around the world in one-fourth of a second, when distance is destroyed and all nations are
jumbled together in one room, the distinction between *home* and *foreign* is gone. Physically the world
is one; that great miracle is wrought. Spiritually it is
at war; that is the peril that faces us. And in over-
coming this peril the noblest spirits of all nations
must stand together. All seekers for the truth are
brothers; the very blindest gropings for truth are to
be encouraged. Goodness is to be welcomed under
whatever flag. In this crisis time is a factor of the

greatest moment. We cannot pause. We cannot wait for a better day. We cannot place physical rehabilitation or economic adjustment ahead of coördination of spiritual forces. From the most practical standpoint either of economics or politics, the spread of Christianity is the one most fundamental and imperative duty of the hour.

Appendix

List of books helpful in making an appraisal of the present-day values in the non-Christian religions of the Orient.

Confucianism

Chu Hsi, *The Philosophy of Human Nature*, translated by J. Percy Bruce. London, 1922.

Dubs, Homer H., *Hsüntze, the Moulder of Ancient Confucianism*. London, 1927.

Giles, Herbert A., *Confucianism and Its Rivals*. New York, 1915.

Giles, Lionel, *The Sayings of Confucius*. London, 1926.

Hsü, P. C., *Ethical Realism in Neo-Confucianism Thought*. Peiping, 1933.

Legge, James, *The Chinese Classics*. Oxford, 2nd ed. rev. 1893-95.

Liang Ch'i-ch'ao, *History of Chinese Political Thought*, translated by L. T. Chên. London, 1930.

Lyon, D. Willard, *Religious Values in Confucianism*. New York, 1928.

Mencius, translated by Leonard A. Lyal. London, 1933.

Soothill, William E., *The Analects of Confucius*. Yokohama, 1910.

Shryock, J. K., *The Origin and Development of the State Cult of Confucius*. New York, 1932.

Wilhelm, Richard, *Confucius and Confucianism*, translated by A. P. and G. H. Danton. New York, 1931.

TAOISM

Fung Yu-lan, *Chuang-tzŭ*. Shanghai, 1932.

Fung Yu-lan, *A Comparative Study of Life's Ideals.* Shanghai, 1925.

Giles, Herbert A., *Chuang Tzŭ, Mystic, Moralist, and Social Reformer*. Shanghai, 2nd ed. 1926.

Giles, Lionel, *The Sayings of Lao Tzŭ*. London, 1911.

Huai Nan Tzŭ, *Tao the Great Luminant, Essays from Huai Nan Tzŭ*, by Evan Morgan. London, 1934.

Waley, Arthur, *The Way and Its Power*. London, 1934.

Webster, James, *Kan Ying P'ien*, book of rewards and punishments. Shanghai, 1918.

BUDDHISM

Fa Hsien, *The Travels of Fa-hsien;* or Record of the Buddhistic Kingdoms; retranslated by H. A. Giles. Cambridge, 1923.

Grousset, René, *In the Footsteps of the Buddha*, translated by M. Leon. London, 1932.

Hamilton, C. H., *Buddhism in India, Ceylon, China and Japan, A Reading Guide*. Chicago, 1931.

Hodous, L., *Buddhism and Buddhists in China*. New York, 1924.

Hsüan Chuang, *Si-yu-ki, Buddhist Records of the Western World*, translated by S. Beal. London, 1884; Boston, 1885.

Hu Shih, "Development of Zen Buddhism in China," *The Chinese Social and Political Science Review*, January, 1932, pp. 475-505.

Johnston, R. F., *Buddhist China*. London, 1913.

Soothill, W. E., *The Lotus of the Wonderful Law*. Oxford, 1930.

Reichelt, K. L., *Truth and Tradition in Chinese Buddhism*. Shanghai, 1927.

GENERAL

Clennel, W. J., *The Historical Development of Religion in China*. London, 1914.

Stuart, Warren H., *The Use of Material from China's Spiritual Inheritance in the Christian Education of Youth*, a guide and source book for Christian teachers in China. Shanghai, 1932.

Weiger, L. A., *A History of Chinese Religious Beliefs and Philosophical Opinions in China*, translated by E. T. C. Werner. Hsien-hsien, Chihli, 1927.

Index of Names